JavaScript
for InDesign
second edition

by Peter Kahrel

creative
PRO

InDesignSecrets

A note from the Publisher:
If you know people who would benefit from this book, please refer them to *indesignsecrets.com/shop*. Thank you!

ISBN: 978-1-950896-01-1

Designed by Ren Reed using Adobe® InDesign®

The typefaces used are Klinic Slab for the body text and Barlow Condensed for the chapter titles. Designed by Joe Prince, Klinic Slab is a contemporary, versatile slab-serif. Barlow Condensed is a slightly rounded, low-contrast, grotesk font superfamily designed by Jeremy Tribby.

Contents

To our readers

In this book, all JavaScript code is formatted with a yellow highlight and in a different font, both in standalone code examples:

```
app.selection[0]
```

and when the it's within body text: `app.selection[0]`. Within the code you'll see that comment text is colored **green** and literal text strings are colored **red**. In some cases, to call attention to them, other JavaScript elements like operators and properties are colored **blue**.

Please contact us at ebooks@cpn.co to inform us of any errors, typos, or broken links that somehow escaped our close scrutiny.

Foreword

Adobe InDesign is like an iceberg: The features you see in the panels and menus are only a small percentage of what's actually available in the program; the rest lies below the surface. If you want to access those hidden riches, you just need to learn three relatively straightforward concepts:

- InDesign's "Object Model" (how the program organizes itself internally and how it names its pieces),

- The basics of JavaScript, a scripting language that uses operators, properties, and other logical bits to manipulate web page and software program features; and finally,

- How to put those two together—that is, how to write JavaScript code that will access and manipulate Object Model components (pages, text frames, and so on).

In *JavaScript for InDesign*, author Peter Kahrel presents these three concepts in his usual clear and comprehensible manner. In fact, you'll find yourself writing your first script within the first few pages. He covers everything from writing and testing JavaScripts, to how to troubleshoot the scripts that aren't behaving well.

Peter is the rare combination of InDesign guru and generous teacher. For years, he has provided the InDesign user community with dozens of free scripts that he's written himself and diligently updated as new versions of InDesign were released. You can browse through them and download them at https://creativepro.com/files/kahrel/indesignscripts.html. Now, in *JavaScript for InDesign*, he shares what he's learned for InDesign users who want to dive in and explore the rest of the iceberg.

I'm sure you'll enjoy the book and reap the benefits for years to come! If you write a great script, please let us know! Post about it in the InDesignSecrets.com forums or email us at info@indesignsecrets.com.

—Anne-Marie Concepcion
co-host, InDesignSecrets.com
InDesign workflow trainer/consultant

1

Introduction

Two things stand between the would-be scripter and an InDesign JavaScript: InDesign's object model and JavaScript. Though both are complex, once a few hurdles are overcome, anyone can start writing scripts fairly quickly. This guide hopes to show that numerous tedious tasks in InDesign can be automated with very simple scripts of sometimes just one or two lines. These simple scripts can pave the way to more complicated scripts. What you need most of all is determination.

To give just one short example, imagine this task: you have a document with dozens of pages, and each page contains one or more text frames and one or more graphics. All these page items are on the same layer, and you decide that the document would be much easier to handle if the graphics were on a separate layer. The task, then, consists of two steps: create a new layer and move all graphics to this layer. Can you imagine doing this manually? Well, the following two-line script does it for you in the blink of an eye:

```
myLayer = app.activeDocument.layers.add ({name: 'pictures'});
app.activeDocument.rectangles.everyItem().itemLayer = myLayer;
```

The first line creates a new layer with the name 'pictures', the second line moves all graphics to that layer. You ask, 'But how do I know that layers are added like that', and 'How do I know that a graphic is in an object 'rectangle'?' Read on – the purpose of this guide is to show how to discover this. Another aim is to show that there are many very tedious and labour-intensive tasks in InDesign which can be solved with surprisingly simple scripts.

This book is intended for people who know InDesign fairly well but do not necessarily know much about scripting/programming. Knowledge of InDesign is necessary; after all, if you don't know InDesign there's not much point trying to script it. Knowledge of a programming language is not necessary (though it helps, of course). I believe that anyone can learn how to write scripts up to a certain level. You don't have to be a mathematician in order to acquire some scripting skills. In fact, many excellent script writers are graphic designers or typesetters or have different backgrounds, as can be seen, for instance, in Adobe's scripting forum. Creating JavaScripts for InDesign is not about computer science: it is about making something work in InDesign, and often that's pretty simple.

In essence, this guide contains three parts. In the first part we deal with Adobe's script editor and the object model, and we show how the object model can be explored using the script editor. The second part outlines the basics of JavaScript. This is not a full JavaScript course but deals with the main elements of the language and gives some examples to get you started. And in the third part we write several scripts. They all essentially handle text. The first few scripts deal with a number of basic text-scripting techniques. This is followed by some scripts that go into various aspects of find and change. I first show how this can be scripted merely to automate InDesign's Find/Change dialog, then move on to show how Find can be used to script a flexible kerning editor. We then take a close look at tables. Though InDesign's tables are quite powerful, some features are missing and we'll show how these can be scripted. In the last section we turn to some aspects of text frames.

All scripts in this book have been tried and tested, and should work as advertised in modern InDesign versions (they should in fact work in versions dating back to CS3). Nevertheless, before trying any script, even those that seem simple and innocuous, always make a copy of your document or try the script on a mock document. Never try out a script on an unsaved production document: InDesign's undo works very well, but you don't want to put yourself at its mercy.

2

JavaScript/ExtendScript

InDesign and other scriptable Adobe applications use a variant of JavaScript called 'ExtendScript'. It's called ExtendScript because it's JavaScript extended with file-handling and XML-processing. ExtendScript is a by now quite old version of JavaScript, lacking various interesting features that were added in recent years, but it's more than capable. InDesign JavaScript scripts are cross-platform: they can be used on both the Mac and Windows.

3

The Script Editor

JavaScript files are plain text files. Though they can be created in any text editor, it's advisable to use Adobe's script editor. It's called the ExtendScript Toolkit (ESTK) and it can be downloaded from the Creative Cloud app. The advantage, as we shall see shortly, is that you can run a script straight from the ESTK: there's no need first to save the script, then to run it from within InDesign.

However, the ESTK is beset by problems on the Mac. There have been various problems in recent years which could make working with it problematic. But more ominously, in the second half of 2019 Apple's latest operating system upgrade will stop support for 32-bit applications, and since the ESTK is 32-bit it can no longer be used on the Mac. This led many Mac script writers to abandon the ESTK entirely and to rely on text editors.

Things look better on the Windows side. Even so, the ESTK is an aging application that hasn't seen any development for many years. It still works remarkably well for such an old application but its age is showing.

The ExtendScript Toolkit

After installing the ESTK, open it. FIGURE 1 shows its default layout. I always have only the edit window and the console open, that leaves more space for script text.

Start a new file (Ctrl+N or File > New JavaScript). At the top left there's a dropdown with application names, in which ExtendScript Toolkit CC is the selected application every time you start the ESTK (FIGURE 1). To link the ESTK to InDesign, select your version from that dropdown (all

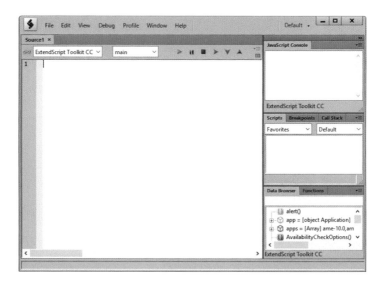

FIGURE 1

6

Adobe applications that can be scripted with Extend-Script are there). Let's now write and run our first script.

To deal with the ESTK problems on the Mac, Adobe created an ExtendScript plug-in for Visual Studio Code. This is a popular Microsoft code editor for Windows and Mac, which can be downloaded for free from https://code.visualstudio.com. The ExtendScript plug-in can be downloaded from https://cpn.co/g/aesdb. The page with this download link includes directions on how to set up the plug-in and how to use it.

If you're on Windows I would advise you to use Adobe's ESTK script editor: it's simpler to install and use and it has its own object-model viewer (see details in the Introduction). On the Mac, do try the ESTK and if it works for you, stay with it while you can. Naturally, when the Mac OS upgrade makes working with the ESTK impossible you'll have to switch to Visual Studio.

5

Hello World!

Make sure InDesign is open. Then start a new script with a new editor window open, and enter `alert ('Hello world!');` (**FIGURE 2**). You can now run the script straight away against InDesign: choose Debug > Run (or press F5) to run the script. A small window is displayed (**FIGURE 3**):

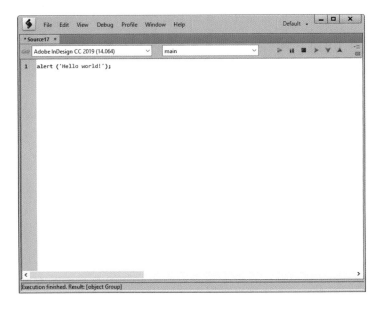

FIGURE 2

FIGURE 3

Saving scripts

Scripts should be saved in InDesign's Script Panel folder, which is in the Scripts folder. The easiest way to find that folder is as follows: open the Scripts panel in InDesign (Window > Utilities > Scripts), right-click the User folder, then select 'Reveal in Explorer' (Windows) or 'Reveal in Finder' (Mac). This opens your scripts folder: (**FIGURE 4**)

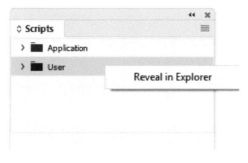

FIGURE 4

Another possibility: open the ESTK's Scripts panel (Window > Scripts), select your application in the drop-down, and click 'User'. The path to InDesign's Script folder is shown at the bottom of the window (**FIGURE 5**).

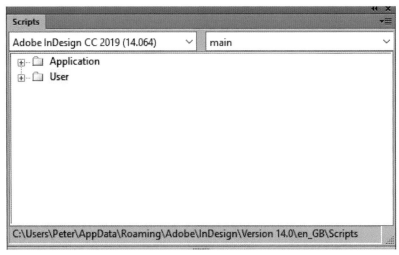

FIGURE 5

On the Mac, to avoid problems with read and write permissions, it's better to keep your scripts in the user folder.

For more details on the ESTK, go to Help > JavaScript ToolsGuide CC. The PDF file that opens contains a chapter on the ESTK with useful information.

Another important part of the ESTK is its object-model viewer (OMV). In this window you can discover which objects are contained in InDesign's object model and what their properties are. The ESTK's object-model viewer isn't particularly popular. There are some alternatives (see the Resources chapter), but for various reasons I prefer the ESTK's viewer and will use it in this book throughout.

But before we go into this we need to get an idea of what InDesign's object model actually is, and the next section illustrates how the ESTK can be used to explore it. After that we'll deal with the viewer and show how to use it.

6

InDesign's Object Model

Fire up the ESTK and press Ctrl/Cmd+N to start a new script file. Make sure that the console is displayed. In InDesign, start a new document, create a text frame, and fill it with placeholder text. Place the cursor somewhere in the text.

In the ESTK, place the cursor in the blank script window, type `app.selection[0]` and run this one line (press F5 or choose Run from the Debug menu). (`[0]` is an index; its meaning is not very important just now.) This one-line script tells you what is selected in the InDesign document. In the JavaScript console, ESTK reports `[object InsertionPoint]`.

This tells us that what we have currently selected is an object of type 'insertion point'. (also known as 'the cursor position'.) Let's experiment a bit further. Go to the InDesign document and select just one character. Return to the ESTK and choose Run again. The ESTK now reports `[object Character]`. Let's try some more: in the InDesign document, select a word by double-clicking it; ESTK tells you that your selection is a word object: `[object Word]`. Go on to triple-click somewhere in the InDesign document to select a line, and run the script against that selection: `[object Line]`. Quadruple-click somewhere in a paragraph, and ESTK says [object Paragraph]. Finally, select the whole text frame in InDesign (Ctrl/Cmd+click) and choose Run in the ESTK; it reports [object TextFrame]. So you see, whatever you have selected, the ESTK will tell you what it is. (If you have nothing selected, the ESTK tells you undefined.)

So far, the ESTK has been telling us what type of object our selection was, but maybe we also want to know what is *in* those objects – in other words, what the contents are. Many objects have contents; let's try a few that we saw just now. In the InDesign document, select once more a word by double-clicking it. Go to the ESTK script and add .contents to app.selection[0], so that it reads app.selection[0].contents and choose Run. As you see, the ESTK now gives you the contents of the word object as text. Try the same with the text frame selected, and the ESTK shows all the contents of the text frame. It makes sense that when you select an insertion point (i.e. you just place the cursor somewhere in the text) and ask for its contents, the ESTK responds with nothing at all. In fact, it does respond quite literally with nothing in an *Alice in Wonderland* sort of way, but, unsurprisingly, you can't see that.

But let's move on with our exploration of the object model, which we earlier described as a hierarchical structure. It is characteristic of hierarchical models for any item to have nodes above and below it – that is, parents and children – apart, of course, from the top nodes (which have no parents) and the bottom nodes (which are childless). The parents are easy to find in InDesign, but the children are a little harder to figure out. We'll start with the parents.

Parents

In the InDesign document, select an insertion point – that is, click anywhere in a text frame with some text in it). Then in the ESTK script window, remove `.contents` and choose Run to run the one-line script to make sure that the object you've selected is an insertion point. Now add `.parent` after `app.selection[0]` so that the ESTK window now has the line

```
app.selection[0].parent;
```

in it. Choose Run, and ESTK says that `[object Story]` is the parent of our insertion point. Add `parent` again:

```
app.selection[0].parent.parent;
```

which tells you that the parent of a story is the document. Does a document have a parent? It does. The following line:

```
app.selection[0].parent.parent.parent;
```

prompts ESTK to say `[object Application]`. You can add still more parents, but they all say that Application is the parent: Application is the top of the hierarchy.

But what about the sequence we tried earlier: character, word, line, paragraph, etc.? See what happens when you try the parent of each. For example, select a word by double-clicking it and try `app.selection[0].parent` in the ESTK. The answer is `[object Story]`. Try the same with a line selected; the result is [object Story] again. So insertion points, characters, words, lines, paragraphs – all these have the same parent: namely, the story. But can we not get from an insertion point to its parent word, or from a word to its parent line or paragraph? We can. In the InDesign document, select an insertion point, and in the ESTK script window, try this:

```
app.selection[0].words.item(0);
```

to which ESTK responds [object Word]. Now try:

```
app.selection[0].words.item(0).lines.item(0);
```

and the ESTK replies [object Line]. You can go on to add .paragraphs.item(0) to get [object Paragraph]. Note that you can also take all sorts of shortcuts; for instance, app.selection[0].paragraphs.item(0) with just an insertion point selected also gives you [object Paragraph]. Conclusion: there are two ways up in the hierarchy: (a) with a generic query using an object's parent property and (b) using specific queries, such as 'give me a certain character's parent word'. In the latter case, you have to be pretty familiar with the object model.

"object.item(0)" versus "object[0]"

In this section on the object model I'll use object.item(n) for consistency within the model; in the sections that follow I use object[n] because is shorter. The two are functionally equivalent.

The examples that we've used so far show that the object model, though transparent, is not always entirely straightforward. Keep in mind that the notions `app.selection[0]` and `parent` are a script's main gateways to InDesign's object model. Many scripts begin by checking what state InDesign is in, meaning here, if anything is selected and, if yes, what is selected. We'll see several examples of this later on.

So far, to address (or reach) an object, we've traveled up the hierarchy by asking for the parent of an object or by asking for a specific object above our starting object. But we can also travel in the other direction and address an object starting from the top of the hierarchy. Suppose you want to do something with the *something-eth* character in paragraph *y* in story *such and such*. You could address it like this:

```
app.activeDocument.stories.item(0).paragraphs.item(2).words.
item(3).characters.item(0);
```

which in normal English says 'of the current application, in the active document, the first story, third paragraph, fourth word, first character' (JavaScript starts counting at zero: the zero-eth element in the word list is what humans perceive as the first word). Try the above line in the ESTK: it should say `[object Character]`. You can check the contents of that particular character with this line:

```
app.activeDocument.stories.item(0).paragraphs.item(2).words.
item(3).characters.item(0).contents;
```

It doesn't always have to be as long-winded as this. We saw earlier that, climbing up the hierarchy, we could take all sorts of shortcuts using the parent object. Going down the hierarchy we can sometimes take similar shortcuts. For instance, the following three lines are equivalent:

```
app.activeDocument.stories.item(0).paragraphs.item(0).words.
item(0).characters.item(0);
app.activeDocument.stories.item(0).words.item(0).characters.
item(0);
app.activeDocument.stories.item(0).characters.item(0);
```

Naturally, the first character of the first word of the first paragraph of the first story (which is what the first line says) is the same as the first character of the first word of the first story (the second line) and the first character of the first story (the third line).

Children

In a way, we have already dealt with children; we could say that anything to the right of a dot is a child, so that characters are children of words, words are children of lines, lines of paragraphs, and paragraphs of stories. Children are still objects, as the ESTK displays them as `[object xxx]`. When a child displays a value, as `.contents` did earlier, we speak of 'properties'. We'll turn to these after dealing with some special parents.

Traversing the object model

Apart from going up or down the hierarchy, we can also combine the two. Assuming we have an insertion point selected in the InDesign document, the following line in the ESTK gives us the second word of the current paragraph:

```
app.selection[0].paragraphs.item(0).words.item(1);
```

`app.selection[0]` is the insertion-point object; we go up a level to the paragraph with `paragraphs.item(0)`; then down with `words.item(1)`.

Three special parents

You've probably noticed that the parent–child relation in InDesign's object model is not perfect. What you thought might be a grandchild is in fact just a child. `paragraphs.item(0).words.item(0).characters.item(0)` is the same as `paragraphs.item(0).characters.item(0)`. And what looks like a grandparent (or even a great-grand-parent) can in fact be addressed as a parent; `words.item(0).paragraphs.itcm(0).parent` is the same as `words.item(0).parent` – namely, a story. More gener-ously, we could also say that InDesign's object model allows a certain degree of flexibility. This flexibility is also shown in three special parent relations: `parentStory`, `parentTextFrame`, and `parentPage`.

parentStory

As we saw earlier, several objects (insertion point, charac-ter, word, line, paragraph) have the same parent: the story. Now select a text frame and run this line in the ESTK:

```
app.selection[0].parent;
```

The ESTK responds `[object Spread]`: a text frame's parent is a spread (in CS3 and CS4 it's a page). Fair enough – after all, a text frame sits on a spread or a page. The function of text frames is to serve as containers for stories; a story is contained in one or more threaded text frames. So what is the relation between stories and text frames as far as InDesign scripts are concerned? Well, this relationship is not entirely intuitive. With a text frame selected in InDesign, run this line in the ESTK:

```
app.selection[0].parentStory;
```

The ESTK responds `[object Story]`. You get the same response when you select a word, a character, or a paragraph; in fact, whatever you select, `parentStory` returns the current story, even when you select a text frame. While this may not be entirely intuitive, it will turn out to be extremely useful. (Note that JavaScript is case sensitive, so you must write commands with the capitalisation as shown here.)

parentTextFrames

The second special parent is `parentTextFrames`. It is used to get a reference to the containing text frame, which you can do with a line like this (you can't use `item()` here; we'll get to that later):

```
app.selection[0].parentTextFrames[0];
```

This returns the first text frame associated with the selection. If the selection is a paragraph which spans two pages, then the paragraph has two parent text frames.

parentPage

This property returns the page on which an object (text frame, button, graphic, etc.) is placed. To get the page of a word, paragraph, or insertion point you need to get that object's parentTextFrame, then that frame's parent page:

```
app.selection[0].parentTextFrames[0].parentPage;
```

If a page item is on the pasteboard, parentPage returns `null`.

In the section on tables we'll meet two other special parents: `parentColumn` and `parentRow`. Both are parents of the `Cell` object.

Collections of objects

Let's pursue InDesign's object world some more and see what we can do with it. Earlier we saw that if you select an insertion point and said `app.selection[0].paragraphs.item(0).words.item(0)` in the ESTK, the response was `[object Word]`. What if we leave out the last index and say this:

```
app.selection[0].paragraphs.item(0).words;
```

Now the ESTK gives us `[object Words]`. Note the plural. What does this object represent? Can we check its contents? Try this:

```
app.selection[0].paragraphs.item(0).words.contents;
```

That doesn't work. ESTK reports an error, saying `Object does not support the property or method 'contents'`. The offending line is highlighted in red; you need to stop the script before you can go any further, so choose Stop from the debug menu (or press Shift+F5). If we want the contents of the paragraph, we need to address exactly that object:

```
app.selection[0].paragraphs.item(0).contents;
```

However, `app.selection[0].paragraphs.item(0).words` gives us a collection consisting of the word objects in the selected paragraph, just as `app.selection[0].parentStory.words` gives the words in the selected story. The indexes that we've been using so far were `words.item(0)` for the first word and, let's say, `words.item(6)` for the seventh one. (In collections we can also approach individual objects from the end. `words[-1]` is the last word, `words[-2]` is the next-to-last word, etc.) In general, using an object name without an index (such as `words`) results in a collection of objects; you pick out one of the objects in the collection by using an index, as in `words.item(3)`.

One useful property of collections that we'll mention here is length, which can be used as follows. To determine how many characters a selected word consists of, how many words are in a paragraph, or the number of paragraphs in a story, use these lines, respectively:

```
app.selection[0].words.item(0).characters.length;
app.selection[0].paragraphs.item(0).words.length;
app.selection[0].parentStory.paragraphs.length;
```

everyItem()

A powerful element of JavaScript in dealing with collections, one eyed jealously by users of Visual Basic, is `everyItem()`. We're running slightly ahead of things now but that doesn't matter. Take for example a text frame that contains two paragraphs. Recall that, with the text frame selected, this line of code:

```
app.selection[0].paragraphs.item(0);
```

returns the first paragraph as a text object. Now do this:

```
app.selection[0].paragraphs.item(0).underline = true;
```

As you see the whole paragraph is underlined. But if we want to underline just the words, we can refer to every word in the paragraph separately. To underline all words in the second paragraph of the selected text frame, we do this:

```
app.selection[0].paragraphs.item(1).words.everyItem().underline = true;
```

As I said, `everyItem()` is a powerful property and we'll meet it later on in this guide several times. For an in-depth discussion of `everyItem()`, see Marc Autret's article.

Properties

All objects in InDesign have one or more properties, and many of these properties are objects themselves. For example, we saw this line earlier:

```
app.activeDocument.stories.item(0).paragraphs.item(2).words.
item(3).characters.item(0);
```

In this line, `app` is an object (the application, in this case InDesign), and `activeDocument` is a property of `app` (one of its many). But `activeDocument` itself is also an object (of type Document), and has a property `stories.item(0)`, which is an object of type Story. And so on. Two other properties we saw earlier are `contents` and `length`.

The value of each and every property can be viewed, and many properties can be set to a certain value. We can try that on our test document:

```
app.activeDocument.stories.item(0).words.item(0).contents =
'One';
```

This line replaces the contents of the first word in the InDesign document with *One*. Leave out = `'One'` and all that happens is that the contents of the first word in the InDesign document is displayed in the console.

Objects can have anything from a handful up to dozens and dozens of properties. An object of type `Word`, for example, apart from the property `contents`, (i.e., the word itself), also has a font associated with it, a font style, a point size, tracking, spacing, superscripting, etc., etc., – in short, everything you can set in the Paragraph and Character panels, and a lot more. Objects of type `Paragraph`, `Character`, and `Line` have similar properties; the properties of text frames include their position and size, number of columns, etc. – again, everything you can set in the Text Frame Options dialog and the Transform panel, and several others as well.

A problem for the scripter – both for beginners and the experienced – is to know which objects have which properties and what these properties are called. All this can be discovered in the object-model viewer. But before we deal with that tool, we need to deal with another aspect of the object model, namely, methods associated with objects.

Methods

In a way, properties are static, in the sense that they describe a state. Methods, on the other hand, are dynamic in that they 'do something'. For instance, many objects have a method called `.add()`, which, as the name suggests, adds an object; these include document, page, textframe, and index. For instance, `app.documents.add()` creates a new document and `app.activeDocument.pages.add()` adds a page at the end of the current document. Methods are listed separately in the object-model viewer, and they can be easily spotted as they have parentheses following them, with or without parameters. To contrast properties and methods, here is an example of each, both to do with capitalisation:

```
app.selection[0].paragraphs.item(0).capitalization =
Capitalization.SMALL_CAPS;
    app.selection[0].paragraphs.item(0).changecase (ChangeCaseOptions.
TITLECASE);
```

In the first line, `capitalization` is a property that can be inspected or set. To read a property, you use the part of the line up to the equal sign. The ESTK tells you what the property is; we've seen several examples of that earlier.

To set a property, as shown here, use the appropriate parameter (or *enumeration*). Here, too, the problem is how to find out what enumerations are possible; again, the answer is that you'll have to read through the OMV.

The second line uses a method, `changecase()`, to change the case of the selected paragraph (this is the same 'change case' that you use from the Type menu in InDesign's interface). Its one parameter, `ChangeCaseOptions`, has four possible values, which you can find in the OMV: `LOWERCASE`, `SENTENCECASE`, `TITLECASE`, and `UPPERCASE`, to reflect the options in the interface.

Note that `capitalization` is a property of, and `changecase()` is a method of, not only paragraphs, but also of characters, words, lines, stories, text frames, etc. All this can be found in the OMV.

You could say that both examples – `capitalization` and `changecase()` – are methods because both 'do something'. There is an important difference, however: `changecase()` really changes text by replacing lower case with upper case, for example, so it changes the content. On the other hand, `capitalization` changes only the appearance of a text object.

7

The Object-Model Viewer

Like the ESTK, its object-model viewer (OMV) is not very popular. There are some alternatives (see the resources section), but I find it perfectly adequate and in fact I prefer it over the alternatives. But as it is a Flash application it will stop functioning some time late 2019, and then we'll all have to use some alternative.

Whichever version you use, the object-model viewer is one of the scripter's best friends: it tells you about the properties that objects have and which methods are associated with each object. You find the ESTK's OMV in the Help menu. Choose it to display it on your screen.

We need to point the OMV to InDesign. The OMV defaults to 'Core JavaScript Classes'; you put it in InDesign mode by picking your version of InDesign, here, 'Adobe InDesign CC 2019 (14.0) Object Model', as highlighted in FIGURE 6. The OMV has three panels of interest to us:

- **Classes** shows the classes (flagged with ⬡) and enumerations (▦). In FIGURE 6, I selected the object Document. In this panel you can type a letter to jump to the section starting with that letter.

- **Properties and Methods** displays the properties (=X) and methods ( ) associated with the object displayed in the Classes panel. In FIGURE 6 you can see some of the properties and methods of the Document object.
- In the pane on the right, descriptions are shown of whatever you select in the Classes and Properties and Methods panes. In FIGURE 6 you can see that I first clicked on Document, then on bookmarks.

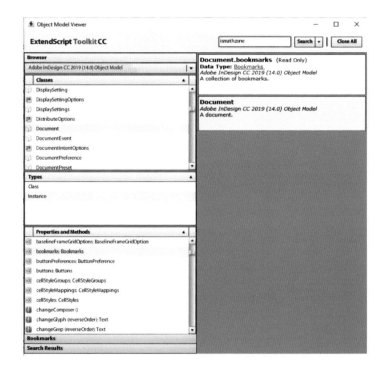

FIGURE 6

The other panels are not of immediate interest to us: for details, see Help > JavaScript Tools Guide CC, end of Chapter 2. Later we'll give some more examples of how to use the OMV to find out how to discover more about InDesign's object model.

Some remarks are in order. First, note that in the Classes panel, the objects use the wrong capitalisation: you should use `document`, not `Document`. Secondly, the classes are sorted case-sensitively, so that `PDF` precedes `Page`. Finally, the object name `Application` is wrong, you should use `app`.

Looking through the Classes panel, you notice that many objects are listed with singular and plural forms – for example, you see `Document` and `Documents`. The properties and methods listed under the plural form are those that apply to the class of documents; an example is `.add()`. The properties and methods under the singular form, `Document`, are about an instance of the class of documents, in other words, a single document. This is an artificial distinction in that the singular form doesn't exist. Thus, to create a new document, we would use this script:

```
app.documents.add();
```

You later refer to this document using `app.documents[0]` (note the plural), and its properties are found under `Document` (singular).

Let's now look at an example of how to use the OMV to find out a particular property, method, or enumeration. Earlier, we saw two examples involving capitalisation:

```
myParagraph.capitalization = Capitalization.SMALL_CAPS;
myParagraph.changecase (ChangecaseMode.TITLECASE);
```

So we have a reference to a paragraph, now we want to apply small caps (the scripting equivalent of picking Small Caps from the Character panel flyout). How do we know about the **capitalization** property? We don't. We consult the OMV. We assume that since we can apply small caps to a paragraph in the interface, we can do so in scripting, too. So in the Classes panel, we go to **Paragraph** (the singular form as we're dealing with an instance of **paragraph**, not the class). We click **Paragraph** and see its properties and methods displayed in the Properties and Methods panel, from **alignToBaseline** to **yOffsetDiacritic**. Now we start looking in the list, expecting to find something interesting under the c. And indeed, we find **capitalization: Capitalization**. Click on that property and the right-hand column in the window shows this:

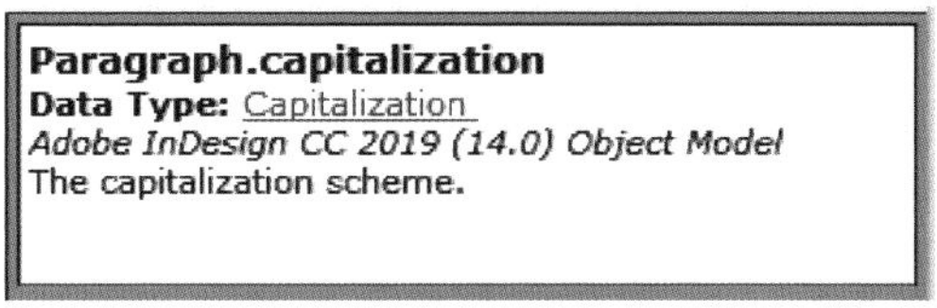

Paragraph.capitalization
Data Type: Capitalization
Adobe InDesign CC 2019 (14.0) Object Model
The capitalization scheme.

FIGURE 7

Now click the underscored Capitalization and the Properties and Methods panel shows the so-called enumerations:

Properties and Methods	▲
=X ALL_CAPS: number, Value: 1634493296	
=X CAP_TO_SMALL_CAP: number, Value: 1664250723	
=X NORMAL: number, Value: 1852797549	
=X SMALL_CAPS: number, Value: 1936548720	

FIGURE 8

Click SMALL_CAPS and a new item is added to the right-hand column that says `Capitalization.SMALL_CAPS`. This tells us that in our script we need to use this form:

```
myParagraph.capitalization = Capitalization.SMALL_CAPS;
```

For the second example, `myParagraph.changecase()`, we follow the same method: select `Paragraph` in the Classes panel to display its properties and methods. Remember, we don't know about `changecase` yet, we're probing. We could suspect that it's a method because it changes the text rather than formatting it, so we could start looking under the methods. But even if we didn't suspect this, we would start looking under the properties, and, failing to find anything of interest there, start looking under the methods.

This case is reasonably clear: we find the method `changecase`. Click it to display the explanation; as in the previous example, it tells us more about the method: `Paragraph.changecase (using: ChangecaseMode)`. Click the link in the explanation to show `ChangeCaseOptions` under Classes; its properties are listed under Properties and Classes. This leads us to the script we're after:

```
myParagraph.changecase (ChangecaseMode.TITLECASE);
```

Finally, to find out which properties and methods are associated with which classes of object, you can use the OMV's Search function, but you must have a pretty good idea beforehand. For example, to discover whether there is a property `capitalization`, and if yes, which classes of object have that property, enter 'capitalization' in the field left of the Search button, then press that button. The pane Search Results will expand and display a list with objects that have the property you searched for.

8

JavaScript

Though the queries we used in the previous section to explore InDesign's object model were in JavaScript, they did little more than give us some information, though in some cases we could actually do something with a single line (e.g. change capitalisation). In this section we present a brief tutorial on JavaScript to outline what it can actually do. We deal here only with those things that are needed to script InDesign and understand scripts. For an in-depth treatment of JavaScript, see *JavaScript: The Definitive Guide* by David Flanagan (O'Reilly). The OMV has a section on JavaScript that provides details on all available functions. For further resources, see the Resources section at the end of this guide.

Some general rules

An important characteristic in JavaScript (which I also sometimes abbreviate JS), easily overlooked and the cause of much misery, is its strict case sensitivity. You must type JS properties and methods exactly as you see them presented in sample code or your script won't work.

Type a semicolon at the end of each line of code in a script. JS ignores returns, spaces, tabs, and any other form of whitespace, so it needs the semicolon as separator between clauses.

Text following // is ignored, and so is any text between /* and */. The former is useful for leaving short comments in a script; the latter can be used for longer stretches of explanation and to temporarily block out pieces of code you want to exclude. In the ESTK, comments are shown in pink to set them off from the script itself (though that can be changed in Edit > Preferences > Fonts and Colors). You can type two slashes, but pressing Shift+Ctrl/Cmd+K is easier: the keystroke adds //~ at the beginning of the selected line or lines.

Many names of JavaScript commands and properties are pretty long, so single lines in a script can be very long as well. Lines can be broken at commas, round brackets, and the = sign. Breaking lines at well-chosen spots can increase the readability of a script; see several examples elsewhere in this guide.

Variables

Variables are items that you name yourself in which you can store information. They are defined using the reserved word `var`. In some places you have to use variables (we'll see those later), but often it's more a case of convenience. For instance, rather than referring to the active document repeatedly using `app.activeDocument`, you can also start a script by storing the reference to the active document in a variable and then use that variable to refer to the document:

```
var myDoc = app.activeDocument;
myDoc.pages.add();
myDoc.indexes.add();
```

Again, this is not necessary; it's just a matter of convenience. When naming a variable, any letter (upper and lower case) and the underscore character can be used. Digits can be used as well, but a variable name must not start with a digit.

In keeping with common practice, I will name most variables using `my` followed by the name of the object type. For example, above, a variable `myDoc` was defined to refer to a document; similarly, I will use `myStory` to refer to a story, and when you see the name `myTable`, you'll know it is a reference to a table object.

Reserved words

There are a number of reserved words in JS – that is to say, words that JS understands in a particular way. In the ESTK, they are easily recognizable as they display in a different colour (the default is blue). Examples of these words are `if`, `else`, `return`, `while`, `function`, `case`, `break`, and `var`. You should not use these words as variables.

Strings

Strings are stretches of text, perhaps no more than one character long. Strings are enclosed by single or double quotes. You define a string as follows:

```
var myName = 'Peter';
```

Strings can be concatenated using the + and += operators:

```
var message = 'This is the first line\r';
message += 'of a message that ends up\r';
message += 'being displayed on three lines';
alert (message);
```

\r is the return character and is used here to force some new lines in the displayed message.

There are numerous string functions. We'll mention a few here that are especially useful. indexOf() and lastIndexOf() return the position of a substring in a string. If the substring is not present in the string, the functions return –1. Here are some examples illustrating these functions (note that JS starts counting at zero):

```
myString = 'Charles Hoare';
myString.indexOf ('e');            //returns 5
myString.indexOf ('rl');           //returns 3
myString.lastIndexOf ('e');        //returns 12
myString.indexOf ('x');            //returns -1
```

The function slice() returns part of a string. It takes one or two parameters. If only a single parameter is used, it is interpreted as 'from', so the function returns a substring from that position to the end of the string. This single parameter can be positive (start counting from the beginning of the string) or negative (start counting at the end). Here are some examples:

```
myString = 'abcdef';
myString.slice (2);   //returns 'cdef'
myString.slice (-2); //returns 'ef'
```

When `slice() is` used with two parameters, the first one is interpreted as the start value, and the second is the (non-inclusive) stop value. The first one must be positive; the second one can be negative. Again, some examples illustrate:

```
myString = 'abcdefg';
myString.slice (1,3);        //returns 'bc'
myString.slice (1,-2);       //returns 'bcde'
```

Strings can be converted to upper and lower case using the string functions `.toUpperCase()` and `.toLowerCase()`:

```
myString = 'james';
myString.toUpperCase();      // returns 'JAMES'
myString = myString.slice (0,1).toUpperCase() + myString.slice
(1);
// returns 'James'
```

Two other useful string functions are `search()` and `replace()`. The first is similar to `indexOf()` (we'll point out the difference in a moment): it returns the position of a substring in a string. The second one, as expected, does a replacement within a string. Some examples:

```
myString = 'Donald Knuth';
myString.search ('Donald');         //returns 0
myString.search ('Charles');        //returns -1
myString.replace ('Donald', 'D.')   //returns 'D. Knuth'
```

These two string functions, `search()` and `replace()`, in addition to strings, can be used with regular expressions (or GREP) as well. We can't go into detail about regular expressions here, but you could do yourself no greater favour than learning some aspects of GREP. It's worth the trouble.

There are more functions with which strings can be manipulated than can be discussed here, but we'll see some more examples elsewhere in this book. For a comprehensive discussion of all string functions, refer to the JavaScript resources mentioned at the end of this guide.

Strings and numbers

Strings and numbers are two of JavaScript's so-called data types (we'll deal with another data type, array, in the next section). In contrast with languages such as Delphi, C++, and Visual Basic, JS is very loosely typed, which means that you need not tell it beforehand that a variable will be used to store a string, number, or array. You can even change the type of a variable with impunity:

```
var num = 4; //num contains a number

. . .

num = 'bear'; //now num stores a string
```

Strings are surrounded by quotes; numbers are not. That means that 4 is a number, but '4' is a string. Though JavaScript is loosely typed, InDesign is not. It is therefore sometimes necessary to convert a number to a string or a string to a number. For example, the contents of any text is and must be a string, so if you want to insert the value of a numerical variable into, let's say, a table cell, you need to convert that value to a string. Here's an example:

```
var num = 4;
myCell.contents = String (num);
```

Conversely, if you read numerical text from a table cell, it is returned as text, even when it 'looks like' a number. So before you do any arithmetic, you need to convert it to a number:

```
var a = myColumn.cells[1].contents;
var b = myColumn.cells[2].contents;
sum = Number (a) + Number (b);
```

If, say, a stores the string `'4'` and b `stores the string '9'`, simply adding up their raw contents results in the string `'49'`, not the number 13.

The `Number()` function can also be used to convert a Unicode value – which is a string, after all – to a decimal value. The following code:

```
var dec = Number (0x0259);
```

returns the decimal value of the Unicode value 0259.

While exploring the ESTK, we saw that you can display the type of an object by selecting that object and running the line `app.selection[0]`. This, however, displays the object type only of InDesign objects, and you can't do very much with the output, such as performing a test. A more general way to obtain an object's type is the `constructor.name`. This is used as follows:

```
app.selection[0].constructor.name;
```

The reason why this is a better method is that it allows you to check your own variables as well. For example, when you run these lines in the ESTK, it will say `String`:

```
var s = 'Nonsense';
s.constructor.name;
```

Since most of the time you'll want to run a script against a particular type of object, this type-check is a good way of preventing scripts from creating havoc in a document. For example, the following test ensures that a bit of text that you want to enter is inserted at an insertion point:

```
if (app.selection[0].constructor.name == 'InsertionPoint') {
 app.selection[0].contents = 'Charles';
}
```

Coming back to the difference between numbers and strings, to test that what you're about to insert is really a string, use this:

```
if (myVar.constructor.name == 'String')
 //go ahead
```

Arrays

Arrays are another much-used data type in JavaScript. They are lists of numbers, strings, or objects. Any list of items separated by commas and enclosed in square brackets is an array (to define arrays informally). You define a new array simply by stating something like this:

```
var myNames = ['Nancy', 'John', 'Betty', 'Jim'];
```

Individual array elements are addressed using the array name followed by an index in square brackets. So `myNames[0]` is `'Nancy'` and `myNames[3]` is `'Jim'`. (Remember that JS starts counting at zero.)

There are a lot of useful functions available to manipulate arrays, of which we'll mention just a few that seem particularly handy. The length of an array (i.e., the number of items in an array) is obtained by `length`. Thus, `myNames.length` returns `4`.

Arrays can be sorted:

```
myNames.sort();
```

Array elements can be combined into a string:

```
myString = myNames.join ('|');
```

This line creates a single string with the names separated by a vertical bar (they can be joined without any separating character or string by using `join ('')` – i.e., an empty string). The counterpart of `join()` is useful, too. For example, the string `myString` we just created can be split into an array as follows:

```
myArray = myString.split ('|');
```

These two functions have many applications in InDesign. A useful example is processing paragraphs in a text frame. To see how this works, create a new InDesign document; draw a text frame big enough to hold about half a dozen names; and type a list of half a dozen names, one per line. Select the text frame or place the cursor somewhere in the list. The following script sorts the list alphabetically:

```
// Check that a story is selected
if (app.selection[0].parentStory.constructor.name != 'Story') {
  exit();
}
// Create an array of paragraphs by splitting the story on
paragraph breaks
myArray = app.selection[0].parentStory.contents.split ('\r');
// Sort the array
myArray.sort();
// Join the array as one string separated by hard returns
myString = myArray.join ('\r');
// Replace the contents of the selected story with myString
app.selection[0].parentStory.contents = myString;
```

A list of paragraphs in InDesign is really one long string with paragraph marks (i.e., Returns/Enters) separating what we perceive as discrete paragraphs. Therefore, if we split that string on the Returns (`'\r'`), we create an array of paragraphs (since we can't sort a string, we need an array). We then sort that array and create a new string by joining the sorted array using Returns (i.e., paragraph marks). (We need to create a string because we can fill a text frame only with strings, not with arrays.) We then fill the story's contents with the new string. (Note: Don't do this with formatted text, it'll become a mess.)

Other useful array functions are `concat()`, `push()`, `shift()`, and `pop()`. `Concat()` concatenates two arrays.

For example, given two arrays, `myFirst` and `mySecond`, the second can be concatenated to the first as follows:

```
var myFirst = ['pen', 'paper'];
var mySecond = ['keyboard', 'disk'];
var myThird = myFirst.concat (mySecond);
```

The returned array, `myThird`, is `['pen', 'paper', 'keyboard', 'disk']`. You can add an element at the end of an array using `push()`. `myThird.push ('desk')` returns `['pen', 'paper', 'keyboard', 'disk', 'desk']`.

With `shift()` you delete the first array element; `pop()` deletes the last element. The following two lines delete the first and the last elements of the array:

```
first = myThird.shift();
last = myThird.pop();
```

After these two lines have executed, `first` stores `'pen'`, `last` stores `'desk'`, and the array now contains three elements:

```
['paper', 'keyboard', 'disk']
```

A formidable-looking but useful array function is `Math.max`, with which you can find the maximum value in an array:

```
var biggest = Math.max.apply (null, [12, 56, 3])
```

`Math.max.min` returns an array's minimum value.

Arrays versus collections

Earlier, especially in our explorations of the object model, we dealt with collections. Here are some more examples of collections:

```
myPages = app.activeDocument.pages;
myCStyles = app.activeDocument.characterStyles;
```

We also saw that individual items in collections can be addressed using indexes and that the size of a collection can be obtained using the `length` function:

```
app.activeDocument.pages[2]; // Equivalent to app.activeDocument.
pages.item(2)
app.activeDocument.pages.length;
```

So what is the rationale for distinguishing collections and arrays? There are three differences between them. The first is that collections can be addressed from the end by using negative indexes, which is not possible with arrays. Thus, `app.activeDocument.pages[-1]` addresses the last page in the active document, but you could not address the last element in our name array using `myNames[-1]`. Secondly, most things in InDesign have a name or can be given one by setting a label. For example, to address a certain character style, you could use the `item()` function:

```
app.activeDocument.characterStyles.item('Emphasis');
```

to refer to that particular character style. This is not possible with arrays.

At the same time, collections can by processed like arrays using indexes, as in:

```
for (i = 0; i < app.activeDocument.characterStyles.length; i++) {
  doSomething (app.activeDocument.characterStyles[i]);
}
```

The third difference is processing speed: arrays are almost always processed much quicker than collections. Depending on the size of a document and the size of the collection you're processing, the speed difference can be dramatic. It is therefore good practise always to convert a collection into an array. Example:

```
myCollection = app.activeDocument.paragraphStyles;
myArray = app.activeDocument.paragraphStyles.everyItem().
getElements();
```

We saw `everyItem()` earlier – it addresses all items in a collection in one go. The JS function `getElements()` splits the object into an array.

For completeness' sake, we mention again that the `item()` function can be used like an index; the following two lines are equivalent:

```
app.activeDocument.pages[2];
app.activeDocument.pages.item(2);
```

Which one of these two formats you use is a matter of taste. I always use the first one because it involves less typing.

Operators

There are several types of operators in JS. We'll briefly outline them in the following sections, including those that we've seen earlier.

Arithmetic operators

The arithmetic operators include:

+	Addition (and concatenating strings)
–	Subtraction
*	Multiplication
/	Division
%	Modulo
++	Increment
--	Decrement

The plus operator (+) is used to add numbers and concatenate strings (`4 + 5` returns the number `9`; `'this' + 'and' + 'that'` returns the string `'this and that'`). Multiplication and division need no comment; they behave as usual. The modulo operator is a division operator, but instead of the quotient, it returns the remainder of the division. In InDesign, this is a useful operator, as it allows you to determine whether an object is on an even or on an odd page: if `myPageNumber % 2` returns `0`, the page is even; if it returns `1`, the page number is odd. For example, the remainder of `5 % 2` is `1`. The increment operator, as in `i++`, abbreviates the operation `i = i + 1` (the decrement operator works in a similar way for abbreviating the corresponding subtraction operation).

JavaScript has a large number of mathematical operators in the `Math` object. Some of these are extremely handy and will be used a lot. For example, to get the larger of two values, use the `Math.max` function (assuming that the two variables `myNum1` and `myNum2` have been assigned a value):

```
var myLargest = Math.max (myNum1, myNum2);
```

This function has a counterpart for finding a minimum value in `Math.min (x, y)`. And earlier we saw a special application of Math.max and Math.min, namely, to return the greatest (or the smallest) value in an array:

```
greatest = Math.max.apply (null, myNumbers);
```

Another useful math function is `round()`:

```
Math.round (12.3)     //returns 12
Math.round (12.6)     //returns 13
```

There are two other rounding functions that round up or down to the nearest integer:

```
Math.ceil (12.3)      //returns 13
Math.ceil (12.6)      //returns 13
Math.floor (12.3)     //returns 12
Math.floor (12.6)     //returns 12
```

For details and further examples of the `Math` object, see the object-model viewer (choose 'Core JavaScript Classes' from the dropdown under Browser').

Assignment operators

The main assignment operator is =, and it is used to assign a value to a variable:

```
var myName = 'Peter';
```

A useful complex assignment operator is +=:

```
newstring += nextChar;
```

This line abbreviates `newstring = newstring + nextChar`. So += is an operator combining addition/concatenation and assignment. You could live without it in principle, but it is in fact useful.

Comparison operators

There are six comparison operators:

==	Is equal
!=	Is not equal
>	Greater than
<	Smaller than
>=	Greater than or equal to
<=	Smaller than or equal to

Note that the = and == operators are different. The first one is the assignment operator used to assign a value to a variable. The second one is the comparison operator used to check if two variables have the same value, or whether a variable has a particular value, as illustrated in the following code.

```
// If myString stores the string 'nonsense'
if (myString == 'nonsense') {
 doSomething();
}
// If current selection is not of type Text
if (app.selection[0].constructor.name != 'Text') {
 exit();
}
```

The operator == is a so-called loose operator, in contrast with the strict comparison operator ===. The difference is best illustrated with an example:

```
a = 12;
b = '12';


a == b;   // Returns true
a === b; // Returns false
```

The remaining comparison operators need no comment.

Logical operators

The three logical operators are these:

&&   Logical and
|| Logical or
!   Logical not

In the first example below, the doSomething() function is called only when two variables have specific values. The second example executes a function if the current selection is a text frame or an insertion point:

```
if (myString == 'nonsense' && hisString == 'hilarious') {
  doSomething();
}
mySelectionName = app.selection[0].constructor.name;
if (mySelectionName == 'Textframe' || mySelectionName ==
'InsertionPoint') {
  doSomething();
}
```

The 'logical not' operator can be used in two ways. Earlier, we saw it used as part of a comparison operator. When used as a negator, it is prefixed to the word it negates. For instance, given a boolean variable `myCheck` (i.e., one that can have only the values `true` or `false`), you check its value as follows:

```
if (!myCheck) {
  exit();
}
```

which means 'if not myCheck'. This is equivalent to `if (myCheck == false)`.

Statements

Under this heading fall a number of control statements for tests (`if`, `switch`); looping through arrays and collections (`for`, `while`); and a general statement, `with`. We review them briefly in turn.

if

Conditional `if` statements are used to test a state and direct the script in a certain direction. The following lines check if anything is selected; if not (i.e., if the selection's length is zero), the script stops:

```
if (app.selection.length == 0) {
 exit();
}
```

When the body of the **if** statement consists of more than one line, it must be enclosed in braces (single lines need not be enclosed by braces but it generally makes code more readable if they are):

```
if (app.selection.length == 0) {
 alert ('Please select something and try again.');
 exit();
}
```

It is possible to use an **else** clause to indicate more precisely what should be done if the condition is not met:

```
if (app.selection[0].parent.constructor.name == 'Cell') {
 alert ('Cell');
} else {
 alert ('Not a cell');
}
```

Several **if** and **else** clauses are possible, but it will soon be easier to write a **switch** statement (see below).

```
if (app.selection.length > 0) {
 if (app.selection[0].parent.constructor.name == 'Cell') {
  alert ('Cell');
 } else {
  alert ('Not a cell');
 }
}
```

The first line is a general check to see if anything is selected at all, the second line narrows the check down further.

switch

Sometimes there are various possibilities to choose from. In such cases, a complex **if** statement can become cumbersome, and it's then time to turn to a **switch** statement. Here's an example that calls a function (which we don't define here) depending on the selection's constructor name:

```
var mySelection = app.selection[0];
switch (mySelection.constructor.name) {
 case 'Character': processCharacter (mySelection); break;
 case 'Word': processWord (mySelection); break;
 case 'Line': processLine (mySelection); break;
 default: alert ('Illegal selection.');
}
```

You need to add the reserved word **break** at the end of each line to prevent each subsequent clause from executing as well. Thus, if you were to leave out the breaks, select a character, and run the script, it would execute all of the three functions and finally display the message 'Not a good selection'. The **default** clause is a catch-all that executes if none of the conditions in the three **case** statements were met.

for

for loops are used to process collections and arrays. The following script converts all items in an array to uppercase:

```
var myNames = ['Nancy', 'John', 'Betty', 'Jim'];
for (var i = 0; i < myNames.length; i++) {
myNames[i] = myNames[i].toUpperCase();
}
```

The **for** loop always has three arguments. The first is the start (or initialisation) value, the second is the end value, and the third is the step value. In the above example the **for** loop reads 'Start at zero, and stop at the value corresponding to the length of the array, incrementing by 1'. You can specify other step values. For example, the following code:

```
for (var i = 0; i < 10; i = i + 2) {
$.writeln (i);
}
```

prints the numbers 0, 2, 4, 6, and 8 in the console.

For reasons that will become clear later, in InDesign you often need to process documents back to front. In that case, you can use a negative step value. This approach is needed when you process the paragraphs in a story, adding or deleting text (we'll see more examples of that when we start manipulating text). To insert an asterisk at the beginning of every paragraph in a story referenced as `myStory`, the back-to-front loop looks like this:

```
for (var i = myStory.paragraphs.length-1; i >= 0; i--) {
myStory.paragraphs[i].insertionPoints[0].contents = '*';
}
```

So, start at the last paragraph and count down to the first paragraph. Indeed, some people always process InDesign objects back to front to be on the safe side, and there's a lot to be said for that approach. As ever, take into account that JS starts counting at zero: if you start at `myStory.paragraphs.length` you'll cause an error, as it is an index referring to an element outside of the collection; you need to start at `myStory.paragraphs.length-1`. To see why the back-to-front approach is necessary, try inserting asterisks from the start of the document:

```
for (var i = 0; i < myStory.paragraphs.length; i++) {
myStory.paragraphs[i].insertionPoints[0].contents = '*';
}
```

while

Like `for` loops, `while` loops can be used to cycle through collections, arrays, and strings. The difference between the two types of loop is that in order to use a `for` loop, you need to know the length of whatever you are processing. With `while` loops this is not necessary. You are much more likely to use for loops, however, as most cyclic work, so to speak, is done on collections and arrays; since you always know the length of this type of object, for loops are the loops of choice because they are a bit easier to write.

But there are situations where you don't know beforehand how many times something needs to be done. Suppose, for example, that you have an overset text frame and you want to fit the frame's contents to the frame by reducing the type size. This could be done as follows:

```
while (myTextFrame.overflows) {
  myTextFrame.parentStory.pointSize -= 0.5;
}
```

This is a crude copy-fitter that reduces the type size by half a point until the whole story fits in its containing frame.

Warning

You must ensure that while statements really test what is happening in the body so that the script can properly finish. If you don't, your script could end up in an infinite loop, meaning that it never stops. You must therefore test scripts with while loops running them from the ESTK so that if something goes wrong you can abort the script. A script that you run from the Scripts panel cannot be aborted; the only way to stop it is to shut down InDesign forcefully.

with

You could live without **with** statements, but they can make scripts easier to write and read. Suppose that, with a reference **myCell** to a table cell, you want to set all insets to zero. You could do that like this:

```
myCell.topInset = 0;
myCell.bottomInset = 0;
myCell.leftInset = 0;
myCell.rightInset = 0;
```

These lines can be formatted as a **with** statement as follows:

```
with (myCell) {
  topInset = 0;
  bottomInset = 0;
  leftInset = 0;
  rightInset = 0;
}
```

This same statement can be stated as follows, which is more compact:

```
with (myCell) {
  topInset = bottomInset = leftInset = rightInset = 0;
}
```

As an alternative to with statements you can apply properties:

```
myCell.properties = {
 topInset: 0,
 bottomInset: 0,
 leftInset: 0,
 rightInset: 0
 }
```

Functions

Functions are bits of JS code that can be executed many times. In that sense, they are scripts within scripts. A simple function is this:

```
function showMessage() {
 alert ('Message');
 }
```

This silly function can be called from anywhere in the script with this line:

```
showMessage();
```

Functions can precede or follow their calling lines (showMessage() in the example). Thus, the following script prints a message in the ESTK console twice:

```
showMessage();
function showMessage() {
 $.writeln ('Nonsense.');
 }
showMessage();
```

The line $.writeln directs the output to the console rather than in an alert.

In scripts with more than one function, the functions can appear in any order. Functions can be directed to use any number of arguments (or parameters). Here is one example:

```
showMessage ('Something for the console');
function showMessage (m) {
$.writeln (m);
}
```

In this example, the function is called with a literal value (here, the string `'Something for the console'`), which is passed to the function body via a variable (here, `m`).

The variable names that you use as function parameters are subject to the same constraints as any other variable. This means that the first character must be a letter or an underscore and that you can't use spaces. Multi-word names are often made by capitalising the first letter of each word and omitting spaces (the so-called camel case), so that you get, for instance, `showMessage()`. Another approach is to use lower case throughout and replace spaces with underscores, as in `show_message()`.

Functions can be defined to operate in two distinct ways. Either they just do something, as in the examples given above (displaying a message) or they return a value (possibly doing all sorts of things as well). As an example of a function that returns a value, the following script prints the percentage one number is of another (here, 9 is what percent of 50?) in the console:

```
function percentOf (x, y) {
 return (x * 100) / y
 }
```

```
var pct = percentOf (9, 50);
$.writeln (pct);
```

JavaScript allows all kinds of shortcuts; some lead to arcane scripts, but others are often useful. One such shortcut is the use of a function call as an argument. For example, in the script given above, the last two lines can be combined into one:

```
$.writeln (percentOf (9, 50));
```

Interacting with the user

JS has a very simple built-in dialog to get users to input something into a script: the `prompt()` function. In its simplest form, it is used like this:

```
var myInput = prompt();
```

The `prompt()` function takes up to three arguments. For instance, the following line displays the dialog shown in FIGURE 9:

```
var myInput = prompt ('Enter a name', 'John', 'Name dialog');
```

Though all these parameters are optional, if you want to omit any, you should use `''` (two quotes, to indicate an empty string); otherwise, the dialog prints `undefined` for message and prompt, and a generic Script Prompt for the dialog's title. The second parameter (`'John'` in the example) is placed in the input field as a default value; you can type anything you want in the input field, which will be passed to the variable `myInput` when you click OK or press Return/Enter.

FIGURE 9

Before you do anything else with the returned value, you must check if the user clicked Cancel (or pressed Escape). If the user did that and you don't check for it, the script crashes the moment you address the variable. This is how you check if the user clicked Cancel or pressed Escape:

```
if (myInput == null) {
 exit();
}
```

If the script passes this point, you know that the user pressed the OK button or hit Enter/Return, so now it is safe to address the variable.

On the reporting side, you can communicate any output to the user via the `alert()` function, of which you've already seen several examples, or you can write things to the console. Unless I write a script for someone else, I prefer to write things to the console, for four reasons. First, what you display in an alert disappears the moment you continue, whereas what you write to the console stays there. Secondly, you can copy the console's contents and paste it somewhere else. Third, the console is scrollable, so there are lists that won't fit in an alert window that will fit in the console. Finally, you must always click the alert's OK button to continue, and when you write to the console that's not an issue.

Fancy dialogs

You can write more complex dialogs using InDesign's dialog system or ScriptUI, with which dialogs for most CS and CC applications can be written. InDesign's dialog system has some limitations. ScriptUI is quite powerful but isn't really for the beginning scripter. For details, see the resources section.

Unicode characters

InDesign and JavaScript are fully Unicode-aware, which is useful, though unfortunately between them they use a perplexing number of different formats. Take, for instance, character `00E9`, the e with an acute accent (é). The format required for this character depends on where you use or see it:

- The Info panel displays this character as `0xE9` (the Info panel omits leading zeros).
- To enter the character in InDesign's text Find/ Change dialog, you need to type it as `<00E9>`.

- In the GREP Find/Change dialog, use `\x{00E9}`, `\xE9`, or `<00E9>`.
- In tagged text files, you need to use `<0x00E9>`.
- To convert a Unicode value to a decimal value, you have to use `0x00E9`, as in `Number(0x00E9)`.
- You can display a character's Unicode value using the `escape()` function, which uses yet another format. For example, `escape('é')` returns `%u00E9`. To convert a Unicode value to text, use `unescape('%u00E9')`.
- To enter a Unicode character in an InDesign document by script, you have to use `'\u00E9'` or `unescape('%u00E9')`. Note that the format `'\u00E9'` is case-sensitive on the Mac.

Despite its comprehensive Unicode awareness, curiously, InDesign has no facility to enter characters by their Unicode values. But here is a small script to fill that strange void in InDesign's user interface (details on the `prompt()` function were covered in the previous section):

```
// Only at an insertion point
if (app.selection[0].constructor.name == 'InsertionPoint') {
  // Display a prompt to get a value from the user
  var uni = prompt ('Four-character unicode value:', '');
  // Check that user entered something and that input length is 4
  if (uni != null && uni.length == 4) {
    app.selection[0].contents = unescape ('%u' + uni);
  }
}
```

The script should really first check if there's an open document and if there's a selection. We'll leave that up to you.

9

Catching Errors

We've mentioned a few times by now that you should always test whether it's safe to let a script do something. Two of the examples we've seen are the following:

```
if (app.selection.length > 0 && app.selection[0].constructor.name
!= 'InsertionPoint') {...
    if (hisString == 'nonsense') {...
```

These two checks are specific: the first one tests whether something is selected and the whether the selection is an insertion point; in the second one we make sure that we do something only if the variable `myString` has a particular value. We use specific tests like these when we are well aware of what could go wrong.

However, we often don't know what could go wrong, or we might run into problems because of various reasons. Trying to list the possible error conditions could be tedious, and besides, you never know if you've got them all. To deal with these situations, you can use JavaScript's general error catcher. Let's force an error. Place the cursor in some text in an InDesign document, then run this script:

```
try {
app.selection[0].contents = 3;
} catch (myError) {
alert (myError);
exit();
}
```

What we want to do goes in the block under **try**. Any
error that occurs during the execution of the clause(s) in
the **try** block are caught by the **catch** statement and the
script passes control to the script code in the **catch** block.

Here, we've chosen to display the error and to halt the
script. You could also decide that at some stage in the
script something could go wrong, but you're not interested to know the problem: all you care about is that the
script gets on with it. In that case you can use a more
general form:

```
try {
app.selection[0].contents = 3;
} catch (_) {
}
```

The error is still caught, but since the block under
catch is empty, the script continues as if nothing had
happened. Because we're not interested in the error but
catch() must have a variable name, I use _ as a filler –
but anything will do.

Try-catch constructions can be applied to any amount
of code: our example has just one line in the block under
try, but it could contain any number of lines of code or
one or more functions. For an example of a script that

makes extensive use of try-catch, see the keyboard short-cut for applying semibold in Chapter 13.

10

Running Scripts

We've seen two methods of running scripts. You can run scripts from the ESTK and from InDesign's Scripts panel (Window > Utilities > Scripts). Both these methods are fine, but if you need to run a script very often, other methods may be more useful.

The first is Quick Apply. To activate Quick Apply, press Ctrl+Enter to show the dialog and start typing the script's name. As soon as the script you're after appears at the top of the list, press Enter to run it. Make sure that scripts are enabled in Quick Apply's list.

The quickest way to run a script is to assign a keyboard shortcut to it. Here's a short description of how to do that. Go to the Keyboard Shortcuts dialog (Edit > Keyboard Shortcuts). In the Product Area drop-down, choose Scripts, which displays all scripts. You'll see several folders; the folder you want is most probably the one called 'Users'. Highlight the script you want to assign a shortcut to and assign it in the normal way, as you would to any other InDesign menu or panel item. The script can then be run simply by pressing that shortcut key. Finally, my favourite way of running scripts is from a small dedicated dialog which I wrote. This dialog works much in the same way as InDesign's Quick Apply panel.

11

Working with Text

With the relevant knowledge of InDesign's object model, some idea about properties, and enough knowledge of JavaScript, we should now set about doing something useful with InDesign's objects and their properties. We'll begin with some aspects of text processing.

Adding, replacing, and removing text

To add text to, let's say, a paragraph, place the cursor anywhere in a paragraph in an InDesign document. Remember that each text object has insertion points. If you position the cursor at the very beginning of the paragraph, you in effect select the paragraph's first insertion point, which in JavaScript is called `insertionPoints[0]` (in fact, the number of insertion points in a paragraph equals the number of characters plus 1, as there's an insertion point at the end of a paragraph as well). By specifying the contents of an insertion point, you add text at that point. So, the line:

```
app.selection[0].paragraphs[0].insertionPoints[0].contents =
'Nevertheless, ';
```

inserts the text `Nevertheless,` at the beginning of the selected paragraph. To add a word between the second and third words, do this:

```
app.selection[0].paragraphs[0].words[1].insertionPoints[-1].
contents = ' marbles';
```

This adds a space followed by the string `marbles` after the second word.

Some caution is needed when adding text at the end of a paragraph. To see why, select a paragraph and do this:

```
app.selection[0].paragraphs[0].insertionPoints[-1].contents = '
last';
```

Recall that `[-1]` refers to the last element in a collection, so `insertionPoints[-1]` is a paragraph's last insertion point. But when you run the above line, the word `last` is not added at the end of the selected paragraph, but at the beginning of the next one. How is that? Well, the last 'character' in a paragraph is the paragraph mark (or hard-return character), which you can see in InDesign by enabling the hidden codes (Type > Show Hidden Characters or press Ctrl/Command+Alt/Option+i to show the hidden characters; you see the paragraph mark as ¶). So to add something at the end of a paragraph, you need to insert it at the one-but-last insertion point, which is `insertionPoints[-2]`.

What about that paragraph mark, anyway? Is that a normal character? It is indeed; in JavaScript, you can refer to it using \r. That means that it is easy to add a new paragraph. For instance, this line:

```
app.selection[0].paragraphs[0].insertionPoints[0].contents =
'\r';
```

inserts a new paragraph before the selected one simply by inserting a Return/Enter character; it's like pressing Enter/Return there.

To replace an object's text, specify its contents. For example, the following line:

```
app.selection[0].paragraphs[0].words[3].contents = 'new';
```

replaces whatever the contents of the fourth word in the first paragraph might be with 'new'. You can replace the contents of text frames and stories, too:

```
app.selection[0].contents = 'Words, my lord, words.';
```

With the cursor somewhere in a paragraph (i.e., with an insertion point selected), the text is simply inserted there. But with a text frame selected, whatever is in there is deleted and replaced with the new text. Clearly, you need to protect yourself against erroneously doing something drastic like replacing a text frame's contents. As outlined earlier in the section on JavaScript, you can easily test if you should really do what you're about to do:

```
if (app.selection[0].constructor.name == 'InsertionPoint') {
  app.selection[0].contents = 'Words, my lord, words.';
}
```

The first line checks that the current selection is indeed an insertion point. If the selection is anything else, the second line doesn't execute.

To replace a whole story, simply say:

```
app.selection[0].parentStory.contents = 'New story.';
```

This, too, is drastic: it could replace hundreds of pages of text in one fell swoop.

Finally, to remove some text, you could set its contents to nothing. The following line:

```
app.selection[0].paragraphs[0].words[1].contents = '';
```

sets the second word of the selected paragraph to 'nothing' (i.e. an empty string). Another method of removing text is to delete the object rather than setting its contents to zero. An example is:

```
app.selection[0].paragraphs[0].words[1].remove();
```

which removes the second word of the selected paragraph. In contrast with `contents`, which is a property, `remove()` is a method.

Inserting special characters

We met a special character earlier, the paragraph mark, and noted that it can be inserted as `'\r'`. Some other special characters are `'\t'` for a tab and `'\n'` for a forced line break. Most other special characters don't have such handy mnemonic short codes and need to be entered using their Unicode values. But it's simple to find a character's Unicode value in InDesign. To find the Unicode value of the right-indent tab, for instance, enter it in an InDesign document, select it, and display the Info panel (Info from the Window menu or F8). In the centre of the panel you see the selected character's Unicode value displayed (in the case of the tab, this is `0x8`). The first two characters in the Unicode value (`0x`) are just a notation convention; what you're looking for is what follows the x – here, **8**. To enter this Unicode value using JavaScript, you do this:

```
app.selection[0].contents = '\u0008';
```

Instead of `0x`, you use `\u`, and the value must be padded with zeros to four positions. Any Unicode value can be read and entered like this.

Styling text locally

Apply styles to text amounts by simply modifying the relevant properties. For example, to italicise the selected word, do this:

```
if (app.selection[0].constructor.name == 'Word') {
 app.selection[0].words[0].fontStyle = 'Italic';
}
```

This can be made a little more clever. Suppose we have to go through a selection of text and italicise a large number of words and phrases. We want to apply italics to a word if we have just an insertion point selected, but if we have any text selected, we want to apply italics to that selection. This can be achieved by the following script: to italicise a word, just click anywhere in the word (or move the cursor to it) and run the script. To italicise some text other than a word, select that text and run the script.

```
if (app.selection[0].constructor.name == 'InsertionPoint') {
 app.selection[0].words[0].fontStyle = 'Italic';
} else {
 if (app.selection[0].constructor.name == 'Text') {
   app.selection[0].fontStyle = 'Italic';
 }
}
```

We've seen the first line earlier. It checks if we have an insertion point selected. If that's the case, the currently selected word (i.e. the word in which the cursor sits) is italicised; if not, we check if the selection is `Text`, and if that's the case, whatever we have selected is italicised. Note that we haven't encountered the `Text` object yet. You have such an object when the selection in your document is not a word, character, line, or paragraph, but just a couple of words or characters. (How do you know that such an object is called `Text`? Well, remember that the ESTK is very obliging: just select a few characters, run `app.selection[0]` in the ESTK's console, and it'll tell you the object's name.)

The script as it is shown here isn't perfect. If you happen to have a paragraph selected it won't work, and indeed, with a word selected, it won't work either. We'll sort that out later. But the idea is clear: before doing anything, make sure that your script won't create havoc in your documents.

Styling text with a character style

Text can be styled with a character style. But to do so, we first need to know how to address one or more character styles. As you can see in the object-model viewer, character styles can be children of the application or of the document. (*Application character styles* are those that are defined with no documents open, and these are placed in every new document. *Document styles* are those styles that were defined in an active document, and they are present only in that document.) We're interested in the styles in the active document, so we try and get a handle on them as follows:

```
app.activeDocument.characterStyles;
```

Run this line in the ESTK and it returns `[object CharacterStyles]`. Looking under `characterStyles` in the object-model viewer, we see that they have a property `name`, which, unsurprisingly, is the name of the style as you see it in the character style panel. To apply a character style to, let's say, a word, you say that that word's property `appliedCharacterStyle` should be the `name` of the desired style object. As you might be asking for a style that doesn't exist, and as you don't want your script to halt on an error, it's a good idea to apply the style only when you've verified that it exists:

```
if (app.activeDocument.characterStyles.item('Strong').isValid) {
    app.selection[0].paragraphs[0].words[0].appliedCharacterStyle =
'Strong';
    }
```

The first line shows how to check if some object exists. All objects have the property `isValid`, which is true or false. In our example therefore the second line executes only if `isValid` returns true.

The script we quoted earlier, the one that applies italics to either a word or to whatever is selected, can be adapted easily to format text with a character style. I used this script a lot while writing this guide:

```
if (app.selection[0].constructor.name == 'InsertionPoint') {
 app.selection[0].words[0].appliedCharacterStyle = 'code';
} else {
 if (app.selection[0].constructor.name == 'Text') {
   app.selection[0].appliedCharacterStyle = 'code';
 }
}
```

Special words (like `this`) are formatted with a character style called 'code'. Rather than applying this style to certain words I just use this script, running it with a single keystroke (see the chapter Running Scripts).

Styling text with a paragraph style

Paragraph styles can be applied in the same way as character styles (from here on, we assume that the variable `myPar` stores a reference to a paragraph):

```
myPar.appliedParagraphStyle = app.activeDocument.paragraphStyles.
item('Normal');
```

This command deletes all local formatting, but leaves character styles in place, so it behaves as if you applied a paragraph style in the UI with the Alt/Option key pressed. To leave local styling intact, you have to use this:

```
myPar.applyParagraphStyle (app.activeDocument.paragraphStyles.
item('Normal', false));
```

In the first example, we set a property (`appliedParagraphStyle`), while in the second example, we use a method, `applyParagraphStyle()`. This method applies a style to a selected paragraph, using the paragraph style as an object (just the style name as a string, as earlier, doesn't work) and a boolean value `false` or `true`, which indicates whether local styling should be deleted. We specified `false` to keep the local styles in place; use `true` and local formatting is removed while character styles are left in place.

Paragraph spacing

Some publishers want half lines of white space between text elements, not full line spaces (between body text and lists, between text and displayed examples, etc.). To set the line spacing before a paragraph to, let's say, 3 points, you can use the following JavaScript command:

```
myPar.spaceBefore = '3 pt';
```

To ensure that facing pages are equally long, these publishers specify that half-lines of white are to be variable; you can increase the space a bit. Often they also specify that the space above certain headings can be increased a bit, so what we want, ideally, is two scripts: one that sets half a line of white, and one that increases the space before a paragraph step by step. Let's first turn to the script that increments the space before a paragraph by 1 point:

```
myPar.spaceBefore += 1;
```

Each time you run this script, 1 point is added to the space before the current paragraph. Note that you can't increment in this script by `'1pt'`, so we assume here for the moment that your measurement system is set to points. (Naturally, this script, like many others, is really handy only when you assign a keyboard shortcut to it.) To reduce the paragraph space, we do something similar:

```
myPar.spaceBefore -= 1;
```

But now we need to be careful: what if the paragraph space is less than 1 point? Try it: the ESTK will produce an error ('Data is out of range'). Ideally, we check the space before, before we decrease it:

```
if (myPar.spaceBefore >= 1) {
 myPar.spaceBefore -= 1;
} else {
 myPar.spaceBefore = 0;
}
```

If the space before the current paragraph is 1 point or more, spacing is reduced by 1 point; if the spacing is less than 1 point, it is set to 0. This same script could be cast in a try-catch construction as well:

```
try {
 myPar.spaceBefore -= 1;
} catch (_) {
 myPar.spaceBefore = 0
}
```

This is just a notational variant. It tries to decrease the space before by 1 point; if that doesn't work, it sets the space to 0.

Now we turn to adding half a line of white above a paragraph. This is a bit more involved as we want a generalised script that figures out what the current leading is and then adds half that above the paragraph. A paragraph's leading is obtained from its property `leading`. You can check this in the object-model viewer, or you can give it a shot in the ESTK. Select a paragraph in an InDesign document, and in the ESTK type this line in a new file:

```
app.selection[0].leading;
```

Quite often it is easier simply to try something. If it doesn't work, you can always consult the object-model viewer later. In this case it works, and the value of the leading is displayed. If the leading of the current paragraph is fixed, the value is printed in the console as a bare number. If, on the other hand, the paragraph's leading is automatic, the leading's value is returned as AUTO.

Now, if the paragraph leading is fixed, you add half a line of white simply by adding half the leading to the space before the paragraph. On the other hand, if leading is automatic, you first need to determine the value of the auto leading, multiply that by the point size (which gives the leading), and divide the product by 2 (to get the value for half a line of white). In JavaScript you do this as follows:

```
if (myParagraph.leading == Leading.AUTO) {
 var myLeading = myParagraph.pointSize * (myPar.autoLeading /
100);
 } else {
 var myLeading = myParagraph.leading;
 }
 myPar.spaceBefore += (myLeading / 2);
```

In the first line we check the state of the paragraph's leading ('if the leading is autoleading'). If leading is auto, in the second line, we get the paragraph's point size and multiply that by the paragraph's autoleading value divided by 100 (e.g. for a value of 120%, we need the multiplier to be 1.2) and assign the outcome to another variable, which we here call myLeading. If the leading is not auto (i.e. it is fixed), we simply assign the value of the paragraph's leading to the myLeading variable. Finally, we add half of myLeading's value to the paragraph's space before.

I use these scripts a lot. In fact, I use six of them a lot: one to add half a line of white before a paragraph, one to add 1 point to, and one to subtract 1 point from the space before the current paragraph. A comparable set of three work on the space after a paragraph. Naturally, these six scripts are assigned to keyboard shortcuts.

12

Working with Tabs

I often need to set tabs in certain types of list. The simplest case is a list of abbreviations, in which we want an em space between the second column and the longest abbreviation in the first column. Here is an example:

CC   Creative Cloud
ESTK   ExtendScript Toolkit
ID   InDesign
JS   JavaScript
OMV   Object Model Viewer
VSC   Visual Studio Code

What we need to do is to measure the length of all abbreviations, determine which is the longest, add the width of an em to it, and set a tab stop in each paragraph in the selection. Here is the script (we assume that there are already tab characters between the abbreviation and the full form):

```
// Make sure we have a proper selection
if (app.selection[0].constructor.name !== 'Text') exit();
// Store the selected paragraphs in myParagraphs
var myParagraphs = app.selection[0].paragraphs;
// Find the longest abbreviation
var longest = Math.max.apply (null, myParagraphs.everyItem().
words[0].insertionPoints[-1].horizontalOffset);
// Determine the width of an em
var em = myParagraphs[0].characters[0].pointSize;
// Tab position: position last letter - position first letter
plus em
var tab = (longest - myParagraphs[0].insertionPoints[0].
horizontalOffset) + em;
// Set tab in all selected paragraphs
app.selection[0].tabList = [{position: tab, alignment:
TabStopAlignment.LEFT_ALIGN}];
// Set left indent and first-line indent
app.selection[0].leftIndent = longest;
app.selection[0].firstLineIndent = -longest;
```

Before running the script, select some paragraphs. (Note that it's not necessary to select whole paragraphs: the first and the last paragraph can be partially selected.) The script first checks if we have a proper selection, then we store the selected paragraphs in a variable (`myParagraphs`), which creates a collection of paragraphs.

To find the longest abbreviation, we look at the horizontal position of the last insertion point of every abbreviation, in other words, the last insertion point of the first word in every paragraph. In JavaScript, that's:

```
myParagraphs[i].words[0].insertionPoints[-1].horizontalOffset
```

This creates an array of horizontal offsets, and we use `Math.max` to get the greatest value in the array. Then we determine the size of an em simply by finding the point size of the first character of the first selected paragraph, then, finally, we can determine the position of the tab stop. That's the value of `longest` (the right-hand side of the longest abbreviation) minus the position of the first character of any abbreviation, plus the value of em. The last step is to set the tab stop in each selected paragraph and, optionally, set the values for left indent and first-line indent. A script like this may take a bit of effort to figure out and write, but it will save you a lot of time.

Another, comparable, example is a list numbered with Roman numbers which need to be aligned on the inner digit or inner parenthesis if the numbers are in parentheses. An example of such a list:

(i) Que tiurorbite cae omnimmo intili consum paris.
(ii) Dec vit.
(iii) Ad facchic ibuntium et ingultora nocae vem pota.
(iv) Videm cortaret quam octus actatil icesendam antero ublica verum consulla perum iam nos.
(v) Ad nia con Itatquidius.

To achieve this, we need again to find the width of the widest number and use that to set, in each paragraph, a right-aligning tab and a left-aligning one; paragraphs start at an en from the number; and we need to insert a tab before the number. The script is similar to the previous one in several ways:

```
if (app.selection[0].constructor.name != 'Text') exit();
var myParagraphs = app.selection[0].paragraphs;
// Get the length of the longest first word
var longest = Math.max.apply (null, myParagraphs.everyItem().
words[0].insertionPoints[-1].horizontalOffset);
// First tab position is longest minus position of first letter
var myTab_1 = longest - myParagraphs[0].insertionPoints[0].
horizontalOffset;
// Second tab position is first one plus en-space -- en is half
the point size
var myTab_2 = myTab_1 + (myParagraphs[0].characters[0].
pointSize/2);
// Enter these tab positions in all selected paragraphs
// and place a tab char at beginning of each paragraph
app.selection[0].tabList = [
    {position: myTab_1, alignment : TabStopAlignment.RIGHT_ALIGN},
    {position: myTab_2, alignment : TabStopAlignment.LEFT_ALIGN}];
// Add a tab at the start of each line
app.selection[0].paragraphs.everyItem().insertionPoints[0].
contents = '\t';
app.selection[0].leftIndent = myTab_2;
app.selection[0].firstLineIndent = -myTab_2;
```

First the script determines the length of the longest number, as in the previous script. That will be the position of the right-aligning tab. We get the second tab position (i.e., the tab position where the text starts) by adding the value of an en space, which is equal to the current point size divided by 2. Then we set the tab stops to the current selection; finally, we insert a tab at the beginning of each paragraph (notice how we use `everyItem()` here), and we set the hanging indents by applying the left indents and first line indents in the selected paragraphs.

13

Some Missing Keyboard Shortcuts

InDesign boasts many keyboard shortcuts, but some are conspicuously absent (for instance a shortcut for applying semibold), and there are a few I use in other applications which aren't available in InDesign but which are useful and not difficult to script. Examples of these are some shortcuts present in many text editors, most notably to swap lines, to duplicate a line or a selection, and to insert tabs at the beginning of all selected paragraphs to indent blocks of text. I'll describe some of them here.

A keyboard shortcut for semibold

The default keyboard shortcuts for applying basic formatting include smallcaps, italic, and bold, but not semibold. Since in most work I have to use semibold rather than bold, the standard Shift+Ctrl/Command+B key for bold isn't much use to me, so I wrote a script and assigned it to Shift+Ctrl+B. Here is the full script (note all the try-catch constructions to make sure that the script doesn't stop with an error):

```
try {
 switch (app.selection[0].fontStyle) {
   case 'Regular': case 'Roman':
     try {
   app.selection[0].fontStyle = 'Semibold';
     } catch (_) {
   app.selection[0].fontStyle = 'Bold';
     }
     break;
   case 'Italic':
     try {
   app.selection[0].fontStyle = 'Semibold Italic';
     } catch (_) {
   app.selection[0].fontStyle = 'Bold Italic';
     }
     break;
   case 'Semibold': case 'Bold':
     try {
   app.selection[0].fontStyle = 'Regular';
     } catch (_) {
   app.selection[0].fontStyle = 'Normal';
     break;
```

```
    case 'Semibold Italic': case 'Bold Italic':
      try {
              app.selection[0].fontStyle = 'Italic';
      } catch (_) {
      }
      break;
    }
  }
  catch (_) {
  // Do nothing
  }
```

The script works like other shortcuts: it toggles roman (or regular) and semibold; it toggles italic and semibold italic; if the current typeface doesn't have a semibold font, then it tries bold. If there is no bold the script does nothing. I've added this script in my keyboard shortcuts as Shift+Ctrl+B, replacing InDesign's standard shortcut.

One of the lines needs a comment:

```
case 'Semibold': case 'Bold':
```

This use of case is interpreted as 'if Semibold or Bold'.

Swapping two lines/paragraphs

This very useful shortcut key is present in many applications, especially program editors such as the ESTK. In some text, place the cursor in a line. Pressing the shortcut key swaps the current line (paragraph, in fact) and the one above it (if there is one). InDesign doesn't have such a shortcut key, but it can be scripted. Here is the code:

```
try {
  var par = app.selection[0].paragraphs[0];
  var previous_par = par.parentStory.paragraphs.previousItem
(par);
  if (par.characters[-1].contents != '\r') {
    par.insertionPoints[-1].contents = '\r';
  }
  par.move (LocationOptions.BEFORE, previous_par);
  previous_par.insertionPoints[0].select();
} catch (_) { }
```

In the first line (not counting the lines containing just **try** and the **brace**) we bind the current paragraph to the variable **par**. The second line binds the previous paragraph to the variable **previous_par**. Then we check if the current paragraph ends in a return: the last paragraph doesn't necessarily end in a return – if it doesn't and we swap it with the previous one, then the paragraphs are combined. Then **par**, the current paragraph, is moved before the previous one, in effect swapping the two. Finally, in the last line you see how you can place the cursor somewhere in a text by selecting an insertion point.

I use this script often when editing and correcting lists such as bibliographies and indexes. Each time the script is invoked, the current paragraph moves up. And because the current paragraph remains selected, it's quite easy to move a paragraph up rapidly.

A script that moves the current paragraph after the next one is useful, too. This is only a slight variant of the above script, and I leave it to you to figure out how to modify the above script. (Hint: replace **previous** with **next** and **before** with **after**.)

Indenting a block of text

Another useful shortcut present in most program editors (the ESTK among them), is the tab key to indent a block of text. It inserts a tab at the beginning of all selected paragraphs. Here is the script:

```
try {
  if (app.selection[0].constructor.name ==  'InsertionPoint') {
    app.selection[0].contents = '\t';
  } else {
    app.selection[0].paragraphs.everyItem().insertionPoints[0].
contents = '\t'
  }
} catch (_) {
}
```

This relatively simple script first checks what state InDesign is in. If the current selection is an insertion point, it inserts a tab at the insertion point – this is the standard behaviour of the Tab key. With any other selection it inserts (or tries to insert) a tab at the beginning of every selected paragraph. If the selection is a text frame, a tab is inserted at the beginning of every paragraph in the frame.

Like the semibold shortcut, I added this script in the keyboard shortcut editor under the Tab key, overriding InDesign's standard key. So now when I press the Tab key on my keyboard, the script is triggered rather than the standard Tab key.

Naturally, we would want to unindent as well. This is slightly more complicated because we must make sure that we delete only paragraph-initial tabs, not anything else. This means that every paragraph must be checked. In addition, because I'm used to pressing Shift+Tab to unindent a block in the ESTK, I want to use the same shortcut in InDesign as well. But Shift+Tab in InDesign inserts the Right Indent tab, so the script should insert that if the selection is an insertion point. If on the other hand the selection is something else, the script should try to delete paragraph-initial tabs. Here is the script; some more comments follow.

```
try {
 if (app.selection[0].constructor.name == 'InsertionPoint') {
   app.selection[0].contents = '\u0008';  // Insert Right-Indent
 } else {
   // It's enough to consider only the first character of each
paragraph
   var first_chars = app.selection[0].paragraphs.everyItem().
characters[0].getElements();
   for (var i = first_chars.length-1; i >= 0; i--) {
     if (first_chars [i].contents == '\t') {
         first_chars [i].contents = '';
     }
   }
 }
}
catch (_) { }
```

If the current selection is an insertion point, a Right
Indent tab is inserted (`'\u0008'`). Then we need to look
at any selected paragraphs. But we needn't look at every
paragraph in full: the first character of each will do. This
line, therefore:

```
var first_chars = app.selection[0].paragraphs.everyItem().
characters[0].getElements();
```

creates an array of the first characters of the selected
paragraphs. We then iterate through the array, checking
if the contents of each array element is a tab character
(`if . . . == '\t'`). If it is, we delete that character by
saying `= ''`.

14

Find and Change

Many scripts work on the result of some find operation, which can be a Text find or a GREP one. We'll start with some basics, outlining how you can automate find-and-replace operations. After that we turn to some more applications of InDesign's incredibly powerful GREP feature.

The basics

Find (and change) are the start and at the heart of many scripts. In principle, scripting offers the same possibilities as the UI does, with one important exception: in the UI, the scope of the search can be set to either of five areas (all documents, current document, story, to end of story, or selection), whereas in scripting, you can search and replace in tables only or in footnotes only as well.

Of the four types of Find/Change available in InDesign's interface, (Text, GREP, Glyph, and Object) we deal with only the first two, Text and GREP. GREP Find/Change is far more powerful than Text Find/Change, but it's a bit more involved so we start with Text and show later how to deal with GREP.

Before you can do a Find/Change, you need to set some options. Each option is a separate line and corresponds with an option in the Find/Change dialog:

From left to right the symbols correspond with these lines:

```
app.findChangeTextOptions.includeLockedLayersForFind = true;

app.findChangeTextOptions.includeLockedStoriesForFind = true;

app.findChangeTextOptions.includeHiddenLayers = true;

app.findChangeTextOptions.includeMasterPages = false;

app.findChangeTextOptions.includeFootnotes = true;

app.findChangeTextOptions.caseSensitive = true;

app.findChangeTextOptions.wholeWord = true;
```

To set all options to false (but `includeFootnotes` to true), use this single line:

```
app.findChangeTextOptions = null;
```

As you can see, the find and change options are properties of the application, **app**. Always make sure that you set these options to true or false so that you know exactly where your specified searches apply: if you don't, you might be in for some unexpected results. The next step, and it is important that you always do this, is to reset the Find/Change dialog, so to speak:

```
app.findTextPreferences = app.changeTextPreferences = null;
```

This clears the Find What and Change To fields and removes any formatting from the Find Format and Change Format panels (again, find and change text preferences are properties of the application). If you don't do this you might inadvertently apply all kinds of formatting.

The third step is to specify what you want to search and what it should be replaced with:

```
app.findTextPreferences.findWhat = 'milk';
app.changeTextPreferences.changeTo = 'yoghurt';
```

The last step is to execute the replacement (we'll deal with format settings later):

```
app.activeDocument.changeText();
```

Where to search

We ended the previous session with executing the replacement as follows:

```
app.activeDocument.changeText();
```

With this line, the replacement is made in the whole active document. There are many other objects to which you can apply text replacements. In fact, you can do text replacements in virtually any object:

```
// Selected paragraph only
app.selection[0].paragraphs[0].changeText();
// Only in a table
myTable.changeText();
// All open documents
app.changeText();
```

As so often, the method `everyItem()` proves useful, too. For example, to do the replacement in all tables in the active document (and nothing but tables), use this:

```
app.activeDocument.stories.everyItem().tables.everyItem().
changeText();
```

Earlier we saw that tables are properties of stories, which in turn are properties of documents, so we need to use `everyItem()` on both properties. Finally, in the interface you can exclude or include footnotes, but you can't do replacements in footnotes only. In a script this is easy:

```
app.activeDocument.stories.everyItem().footnotes.everyItem().
texts[0].changeGrep();
```

You may wonder why `texts[0]` is there. Well, I first tried this line without it:

```
app.activeDocument.stories.everyItem().footnotes.everyItem().
changeGrep();
```

as with text frames, tables, and other objects, but that didn't work. So I tried it with `texts[0]`, which worked fine. You'll find from time to time that you need to use trial-and-error methods to arrive at the correct code.

Format settings

Let's now turn to format settings. As in the UI, you can specify format settings for both the find and the replace parameters. To search for superscripted 'th' and replace it with non-superscripted 'th', you do this:

```
app.findChangeTextOptions.wholeWord = true;
app.findTextPreferences = app.changeTextPreferences = null;
app.findTextPreferences.findWhat = 'th';
app.findTextPreferences.position = Position.SUPERSCRIPT;
app.changeTextPreferences.position = Position.NORMAL;
app.activeDocument.changeText();
```

In effect, you remove the superscript formatting. The OMV shows you which formatting can be used in the find and change text preferences. In general, whatever can be assigned to text (characters, words, paragraphs), can be specified for the find and change preferences as well.

Setting preferences is additive; that is to say that when you set a preference, it is added to any previously set preferences (this explains why you have to reset preferences to **null** at the beginning of each script or function that perform a replacement). The following lines set the search to find anything that is italic, underlined, and in small capitals.

```
app.findTextPreferences = app.changeTextPreferences = null;
app.findTextPreferences.fontStyle = 'Italic';
app.findTextPreferences.underline = true;
app.findTextPreferences.capitalization = Capitalization.
SMALL_CAPS
```

Text searches support the same wildcards that are available in the UI. Thus to apply a different font to digits, use this:

```
app.findTextPreferences = app.changeTextPreferences = null;
app.findTextPreferences.findWhat = '^9';
app.changeTextPreferences.appliedFont = 'Times New Roman\
Regular';
app.activeDocument.changeText();
```

Finally, to search Unicode values, use the format <XXXX> or \uXXXX. For example, to find the eng (ŋ) character, Unicode 014B, use either of the following two lines:

```
app.findTextPreferences.findWhat = '<014B>';
app.findTextPreferences.findWhat = '\u014B';
```

To conclude this section, here is a script that can be used as the basis of a script to replace recurring things. In a way it is a (very much) simplified version of the Find-ChangeByList script that ships with InDesign.

```
// Set some options, add any that are needed
app.findChangeTextOptions.includeFootnotes = true;
app.findChangeTextOptions.caseSensitive = true;
app.findChangeTextOptions.wholeWord = true;
app.findTextPreferences = app.changeTextPreferences = null;

replace ('one', 'un');
replace ('two', 'deux');
replace ('three', 'trois');
// etc. etc.
```

```
function replace (myFind, myReplace) {
app.findTextPreferences.findWhat = myFind;
app.changeTextPreferences.changeTo = myReplace;
app.activeDocument.changeText();
}
```

All you need to do to make it suitable for yourself is to change the function calls `replace ('one', 'two')` etc. with whatever you want to find and replace.

We'll leave the find-and-change type of script here, because it is essentially not much more than an automation of what you can do with the Find/Change dialog in the UI. Instead, we'll turn to just the find command and show how the results can be used.

Finding things

So far we've used commands like `app.activeDocument. changeText()` to find and change pieces of text. But often we want just to find things. There is a separate method for this; an example is:

```
app.findChangeTextOptions.includeFootnotes = true;
app.findChangeTextOptions.caseSensitive = true;
app.findChangeTextOptions.wholeWord = true;
app.findTextPreferences = null;
app.findTextPreferences.findWhat = 'elusive';
app.activeDocument.findText();
```

As always, we have to start with setting some options and resetting the preferences. Then we set the text to be found and execute the search. In the form given here, InDesign does find whatever needs to be found, but you can't do anything with it. In order to do something with what is found, you have to capture it. For example:

```
var myFound = app.activeDocument.findText();
```

The first question is, 'What exactly does InDesign find?' To get an idea of this we'll use the ESTK to investigate, much like we did earlier when we explored InDesign's object model. First create an InDesign document, draw a text frame, and enter the letter 'e' a few times: type a word that consists of six 'e's, italicise the second character, and underline the third one. Next, in the ESTK, type the following lines in a new ESTK file and run this script (for clarity, we'll bother only with the necessary options):

```
app.findChangeTextOptions.wholeWord = false;
app.findTextPreferences = null;
app.findTextPreferences.findWhat = 'ee';
myFound = app.activeDocument.findText();
```

(Don't use var before myFound, it suppresses sensible output in the console.) We catch the result of the search and call that result myFound. In the console, you see this:

```
[object Text],[object Text],[object Text]
```

Aha – InDesign finds not text, but text objects. And what kind of thing is myFound? Add this line to the script:

```
myFound.constructor.name;
```

and run the script again: the console says Array. So findText() returns an array, in this case an array of text objects. As we saw in the JavaScript introduction, arrays have length. Remove the line `myFound.constructor.name` and add this line:

```
myFound.length;
```

and run the script again. ESTK answers 3, the number of items in the array. Since `myFound` is an array, we can address its individual members. Remove the last line of the script and add this:

```
myFound[0].contents;
```

As before, we address items in an array using an index in brackets. The line here prompts the ESTK to respond 'ee', the actual contents of the first text object. Remove this last line and add this one:

```
myFound[1].characters[0].underline
```

which amounts to asking 'Is the first character of the second text object underlined?' ESTK says `true` (which is its way of saying 'yes'). This, and further experiments, shows that search results are objects that can be treated like any other object. In the next few sections, we'll give some examples of this.

A kerning editor

In contrast with several other typesetting applications, InDesign has no kerning editor to adjust poorly kerned character pairs and character pairs that the font designer hadn't bothered to kern at all. If you take your spacing seriously, you have to do something about sorting out your own kerning adjustments. With a bit of effort you can script kerning; after all, kerning two characters is just removing or adding a bit of space between two characters. Moreover, a custom-made kerning script can adjust the spacing of characters from different fonts, which is impossible to implement in the application or a font (italic *d* and *f* followed by a roman parenthesis are notorious cases in point). Optical kerning is not always an option, as its results are variable, and setting your own kerning gives you much more control. And as you can't set specific kerning values in the 'Find/Change' dialog in InDesign, it's not possible to kern using search and replace, so we need to script it.

We'll tackle this by setting the kerning value between pairs of characters, which is what you would do in the interface: position the cursor between two characters and press Alt/Opt+left arrow to kern the two characters closer together. The object between two characters is an insertion point, and, as we can find out in the OMV, insertion points have a property `kerningValue`. To make sure that we're on the right track, draw a small text frame in an InDesign document, enter any two letters, and position the cursor between them. Then run this script:

```
app.selection[0].kerningValue = -100;
```

You should see the two characters creep together; if that's the case, you know that this is the way to do it. The script, therefore, is essentially a list of character pairs with their kerning value. So we first need to identify those characters and determine a good kerning value. Some problem pairs in a font I often use, Minion Pro, are a hyphen with some uppercase letters (-T, -V, -W). These look pretty horrible, and their kerning needs to be adjusted. Let's write a script that fixes the -T pair (we'll generalise it later when we have a version that deals correctly with one pair). First determine a good kerning value for -T: type -T in an InDesign document using the font you want to kern, place the cursor between the two characters, and press Alt/Option+left arrow to kern the hyphen and the T together. I found that –100 works well for Minion Pro Regular.

The script first needs to find all instances of -T and assign the found array to a variable:

```
// Set the necessary options
app.findChangeTextOptions.includeFootnotes = true;
app.findChangeTextOptions.caseSensitive = true;
app.findChangeTextOptions.wholeWord = false;
// Reset the preferences
app.findTextPreferences = null;
// Set the preferences
app.findTextPreferences.appliedFont = 'Minion Pro';
app.findTextPreferences.fontStyle = 'Regular';
app.findTextPreferences.findWhat = '-T';
var myPairs = app.activeDocument.findText();
```

The variable `myPairs` now stores an array consisting of all text objects whose contents is -T. To set the kerning value between the two characters, we specify a property of the insertion point between the hyphen and the T, in each text object. Remember that our two-character objects have three insertion points, one before and after the hyphen, and one following the T. The insertion point we need to modify is therefore the second one (number 1 in JavaScript). We'll use a `for` loop to work our way through the array:

```
for (var i = 0; i < myPairs.length; i++) {
 myPairs[i].insertionPoints[1].kerningValue = -100;
}
```

Now, there are more kern pairs to handle, and we don't want to write out the `for` loop for each pair. Instead, we put most of the work in a function. Since we're dealing with roman type, we'll call it `roman_roman` (to distinguish it from another function, `italic_roman`, which we'll do later). The complete script follows:

```
// Set the necessary options
app.findChangeTextOptions.includeFootnotes = true;
app.findChangeTextOptions.caseSensitive = true;
app.findChangeTextOptions.wholeWord = false;
// Reset the preferences
app.findTextPreferences = null;
// Set the preferences
app.findTextPreferences.appliedFont = 'Minion Pro';
app.findTextPreferences.fontStyle = 'Regular';


roman_roman ('-A', -40);
roman_roman ('-V', -80);
roman_roman ('-W', -80);
roman_roman ('7^=', -60);    // 7 followed by en dash
roman_roman ('7,', -60);    // 7 followed by comma
```

```
function roman_roman (kPair, kValue) {
  // Find all instances of kPair
  app.findTextPreferences.findWhat = kPair;
  var myPairs = app.activeDocument.findText();
  // Insert the kerning value between first and second character
  for (var i = 0; i < myPairs.length; i++) {
    myPairs[i].insertionPoints[1].kerningValue = kValue;
  }
}
```

As you can see, most of the work is now relegated to the function. We define the function with two parameters: the pair to be kerned and the kerning value. It is easy to add any new kerning pairs: Determine the optimal kerning between two characters and simply add a line calling the function. Each time you add a kerning pair you need to run the script, but setting the same kerning value for certain character pairs repeatedly is no problem: existing kerning values are replaced, not added to.

We now turn to something slightly more complicated: kerning an italic character followed by a roman one. As in most fonts, in Minion Pro problematic pairs are, among others, *d*, *f*, *l*, and *t* followed by a roman parenthesis, and *e*, *t*, and *s* followed by a colon. To handle these, we define a new function:

```
function italic_roman (kPair, kValue)          {
  app.findTextPreferences.findWhat = kPair;
  var myPairs = app.activeDocument.findText();
  for (var i = 0; i < myPairs.length; i++) {
    // if 1st char is italic and 2nd roman
    if (myPairs[i].characters[0].fontStyle == 'Italic' &&
myPairs[i].characters[1].fontStyle == 'Regular') {
        myPairs[i].insertionPoints[1].kerningValue = kValue;
    }
  }
}
```

Again, notice that the objects in the collection gathered by `findText()` can be treated like any other object. The function works in virtually the same way as the `roman_roman` function; its extra work is checking that the first character of every found pair is italic and the second, roman.

To get this function to work in the other script, add the following lines to the script given earlier (one line of which is repeated here):

```
roman_roman ('7,', -60);      // 7 followed by comma
// Reset the font style in the find preferences
app.findTextPreferences.fontStyle = null;
italic_roman ('d)', 35);
italic_roman ('f)', 180);
italic_roman ('l)', 60);
italic_roman ('t)', 60);
italic_roman ('e:', 50);
italic_roman ('t:', 40);
italic_roman ('s:', 50);
```

Then insert the `italic_roman` function below the `roman_roman` function. The line that resets the font style is necessary, since up to that point the script was looking for the Regular font style, but should start looking for any font style now.

All kinds of other spacing problems can be solved in this way. For example, I often have documents in which uppercase letters are followed by a subscripted index, such as V_3. Clearly, there is too much space between the V and the following subscript. This, too, is easy to correct. We define the function `regular_sub()`, which checks if the first of a character pair's position is normal and the second, subscript:

```
function regular_sub (kPair, kValue) {
app.findTextPreferences.findWhat = kPair;
var myPairs = app.activeDocument.findText();
for (var i = 0; i < myPairs.length; i++) {
  if (myPairs[i].characters[0].position == Position.NORMAL &&
            myPairs[i].characters[1].position == Position.
SUBSCRIPT) {
      myPairs[i].insertionPoints[1].kerningValue = kValue;
  }
 }
}
```

You can call the function using a wildcard in the search argument, as follows:

```
regular_sub ('V^9', -100)
```

This call handles all instances of a capital V followed by any digit.

Find/Change with GREP

InDesign's GREP feature is very powerful. If you don't know GREP you can't do yourself a greater favour than getting to know it to some extent. For detailed information and an extended tutorial on GREP in InDesign, see the ebook I wrote. In what follows I assume that you're somewhat familiar with InDesign's GREP.

In InDesign's interface, the GREP tab in the Find/Change dialog is similar to the Text tab. This similarity is reflected in scripting: GREP find and replace is virtually the same as text, the difference being, naturally, that in GREP find and change you use GREP expressions rather than text. As there are so many similarities, we'll deal with the differences only.

The options available in scripting correspond with those in the Find/Change dialog:

From left to right, the symbols correspond with the following scripted options:

```
app.findChangeGrepOptions.includeLockedLayersForFind = true;
app.findChangeGrepOptions.includeLockedStoriesForFind = true;
app.findChangeGrepOptions.includeHiddenLayers = true;
app.findChangeGrepOptions.includeMasterPages = false;
app.findChangeGrepOptions.includeFootnotes = true;
```

The options can be reset using one command:

```
app.findChangeGrepOptions = null;
```

This sets includeFootnotes to true, the other options to false.

As with Text find and replace, you must reset the preferences before you do anything else:

```
app.findGrepPreferences = app.changeGrepPreferences = null;
```

Otherwise, whatever you can do with Text find and replace, you can do with GREP as well. One important thing to remember is that the backslash must be escaped. For example, if you have a GREP expression like \u\u+, you should use that in a script as follows:

```
app.findGrepPreferences.findWhat = '\\u\\u+';
```

Expressions with many backslashes can become difficult to read because of all the escaping, and an alternative format is then much clearer:

```
app.findGrepPreferences.findWhat = /\u\u+/.source;
```

Lower-casing acronyms with GREP

A frequent complaint in the user-to-user forums is that you can't change the capitalisation of text using GREP searches. For instance, in a text in which acronyms are in capitals (UNICEF, EIB) you can find these acronyms and you can apply smallcaps to them, but you can't convert them to lower case. In some cases this is not a problem, as the feature OpenType AllSmallCaps uses the correct glyphs. But if you're working with a font that doesn't have that feature, then you can't use GREP for acronyms. But this problem can be solved relatively easily with a script:

```
app.findGrepPreferences = app.findChangeGrepOptions = null;
app.findGrepPreferences.findWhat = '\\u\\u+';
var myFound = app.activeDocument.findGrep();
for (var i = 0; i < myFound.length; i++) {
 myFound[i].contents = myFound[i].contents.toLowerCase();
 myFound[i].capitalization = Capitalization.SMALL_CAPS;
 }
}
```

As always, we first set any options we need and we clear the preferences. The GREP expression needed to find any sequence of two or more capitals is \u\u+, which, again should be written as '\\u\\u+' in the script. We search the active document and assign the array of search results in the variable myFound. Then we iterate through the array, replacing the contents of each found item with itself converted to lower case. We also apply smallcaps; you could apply a character style instead if necessary.

15

Tables

InDesign's tables are pretty powerful and there's plenty of use for them. However, there are some gaps – such as the inability to snap columns to their contents – but fortunately, tables are also relatively easy to script. In this section we'll go into some details of table scripting.

Anatomy of a table

A table consists of columns and rows. Tables have many properties, some of which we list here, as we'll use them a lot. With a reference `myTable` to a table, here are a few examples of some of the table's many available properties (consult the OMV for full details):

```
myTable.columns
myTable.rows
myTable.cells// All cells in the table
myTable.columns[n].cells     // All cells in column n
myTable.rows[n].cells// All cells in row n
myTable.columns[n].cells[p]   // Cell p in column n
myTable.rows[n].contents     // Contents of a row returns an
array
myTable.columns[n].cells[p].contents
```

As you can see, you can address all cells in a table, all cells in a column, or all cells in a row. Apart from that, you can also address individual cells. In a table, each cell has a name in the form of what is by now a standard way of referencing cells – namely, the column and row number separated by a colon. As is so often true in InDesign, you can address a certain object in different ways. Thus, the following lines refer to the same cell:

```
myTable.cells.item('3:0')
myTable.rows[0].cells[3]
myTable.columns[3].cells[0]
```

Each refers to the fourth cell in the first row (or the first cell in the fourth column). Cells have two special parent properties: `parentColumn`, which returns a cell's column, and `parentRow`, which returns a cell's row. Thus, if you have a reference `myCell` to a cell, this code returns the cell's column as an object:

```
myCell.parentColumn
```

We'll make good use of these properties later on.

Getting a reference to a table

For the time being we'll deal with just one table at a time, namely, the selected table (later we'll go into batch-processing tables). As most of what we're about to do is valid only in tables, we want to make sure that we are indeed in one. To find out if you're in a table, check what is selected.

If you have an insertion point selected in a table, the selection's parent is an object of type `Cell`; if you have a

cell selected, the selection's parent is the table. So return-
ing the selection's parent or grandparent returns the table
as an object. The following function does that, or displays
an error message if you're not in a table:

```
function getTable() {
  if (app.selection.length > 0) { // Proceed only if something is
selected
    var mySelection = app.selection[0];
    if (mySelection.parent.constructor.name == 'Table') {
      return mySelection.parent;
    } else if (mySelection.parent.parent.constructor.name ==
'Table') {
      return mySelection.parent.parent;
    }
  }
  alert ('Cursor not in a table\ror illegal selection.');
  exit();
}
```

The function returns the currently selected table as an
object or displays a message in case it can't get hold of a
table from the current selection.

Snapping columns

Though InDesign's tables are very good, there are nevertheless some gaps. Most of these, however, can be filled
with scripts; one example is a function to snap columns
to their contents, either to the width of the contents of
the widest cell or to that value plus (often) an em. We'll
begin with the function that snaps the selected column.

The first thing we want to know is which column is selected. This is simple in principle, but as always, we need to check what the selection is. Getting a reference to a column is similar to getting a reference to a table:

```
function getColumn() {
 if (app.selection.length > 0) {
   var mySelection = app.selection[0];
   if (mySelection.parent.constructor.name == 'Cell') {
     return mySelection.parent.parentColumn;
   } else if (mySelection.constructor.name == 'Cell') {
     return mySelection.parentColumn;
   }
 }
 alert ('Cursor not in a table\ror illegal selection');
 exit();
 }
```

Now that we have a reference to the selected column, we can turn to the function that snaps it. (Note again that 'selected column' means the column in which the cursor is, not to any block selection.) What we need to do is (a) widen the column to ensure that the contents of each cell fits on one line, then (b) get the value of the widest cell. The length of the contents of a cell is found by taking the difference of the position of the horizontal positions of the last and first insertion points. The horizontal position of a character can be obtained by its insertion point's horizontalOffset, so the widest cell is the one with the biggest value of the horizontal offset of the last character (recall that we used a similar method in the script for

setting tab stops, see the Working with Tabs chapter).
(I assume here that all cell insets are zero and that optical
margin alignment is disabled as that can lead to unpre-
dictable results.) Here is the function:

```
function snapColumn (myColumn) {
   // Get the size of em space
   var em = myColumn.cells[0].insertionPoints[0].pointSize;
   myColumn.width = '5cm'; // Or use something like '3i' for 3
inches
   // Get horizontal offset of last insertion point in each cell
   var myRightPosArray = myColumn.cells.everyItem().
insertionPoints[-1].horizontalOffset;
   // Find the biggest value
   var longest = Math.max.apply (null, myRightPosArray);
   // Get position of left side of column
   var myLeftPos = myColumn.cells[0].insertionPoints[0].
horizontalOffset;
   // Set column width
   myColumn.width = ((longest - myLeftPos) + em);
}
```

In the first line, we determine the size of the type
in order to set the space between columns. Then the
selected column is set (arbitrarily) to a width of 5 cm
(could be 5 inches – any value will do that's big enough to
get the contents of all cells on one line). Now we need to
find the cell with the widest contents. We do that by comparing the horizontal offsets of the last insertion points
in each cell. This is easily done using the everyItem()
function, which gives us an array of offsets (which are

numbers). To find the biggest of these numbers, we use the formidable-looking `Math.max.apply`. Finally, we get the horizontal offset of the first insertion point in a cell (which is the same for all cells in the column), deduct that from the biggest value we found, and set the selected column to that difference plus the desired space (here, an em space).

The complete script is listed here:

```
function getColumn() {
  /* as defined */
}
function snapColumn (myColumn) {
  /* as defined */
}
snapColumn (getColumn());
```

To snap all columns in a table, we simply process all columns using a `for` loop. First we need a reference to the table, and then we handle each column in turn:

```
var myTable = getTable();
var myColumns = myTable.columns.everyItem().getElements();
for (var i = 0; i < myColumns.length; i++) {
  snapColumn (myColumns[i]);
}
```

Align on units

Another useful function aligns a column of numbers on their units, with the first digit of the longest number at the left edge of the column. What I mean by this is best illustrated by an example. Take this table:

One	Two
Pencils	12345
Biros	678
Paper	9101

There is no real provision for setting columns of figures like this. The quickest way to do this in the UI is to set a character-aligned tab stop at the widest item, using a character that's not used in the column, such as '|'. This is tedious work that can be handled with a script. As this type of alignment usually applies to only part of a column, we'll have the script work on a range of selected cells. Here is the script:

```
    var mySelection = app.selection[0];
    if (mySelection.constructor.name != 'Cell') exit();
    // Get the horizontal offset of the last insertion point in each
cell
    var myOffsets = mySelection.cells.everyItem().insertionPoints[-1].
horizontalOffset;
    // Find the biggest value
    var widest = Math.max.apply (null, myOffsets);
    // Get position of left side of column
    var myLeftpos = mySelection.cells[0].insertionPoints[0].
horizontalOffset;
    var tab_position = widest - myLeftpos;
    mySelection.paragraphs.everyItem().tabList = [{
     position: tab_position,
     alignment: TabStopAlignment.CHARACTER_ALIGN,
     alignmentCharacter: '|'
    }];
```

The script is in principle similar to the column snapper;
it collects the position of the last insertion point of each
selected cell, finds the largest value, and subtracts from
this the horizontal position of the first insertion point of
a cell. This difference is used to set the position of the
tab stop at each paragraph. The tab stop's type is set as
alignment tab, and the alignment character is set to the
pipe symbol.

Shading cells

Shading is cells pretty cumbersome work, so a script
would be useful. In the script below, the first block of
lines check that what we have selected is a cell. If it is, the

script sets the selection's colour and tint. The script works with an insertion point selected somewhere in a cell or with one or more cells selected, so that you can shade a single cell or a range of cells. As different percentages of shading can be required at different occasions, we'll let the script ask for input:

```
function inTable (sel) {
  try {
    return (sel.length > 0) &&
      (sel[0].constructor.name == 'Cell' || sel[0].parent.
constructor.name == 'Cell');
  } catch (_) {
    exit();
  }
}
if (inTable (app.selection)) {
  var mySelection = app.selection[0];
  if (mySelection.parent.constructor.name == 'Cell') {
    mySelection = mySelection.parent;
  }
  // Show prompt dialog, set default to 20 (percent shading)
  var myTint = prompt ('Enter a tint', 20);
  if (myTint != null) {  // If not Escape pressed or Cancel
clicked
    mySelection.fillColor = 'Black';
    mySelection.fillTint = Number (myTint);
  }
}
```

Note first that we must make sure that the script works only in a table: The properties `fillColor` and `fillTint` can be applied to text, too. We tested for tables in an earlier script, but there we wanted to return the table as an object, which is a bit more complicated; here we simply test if we're in a table.

Summing numbers in columns

I wrote this little script a while ago more as a joke than anything else, but it actually has come in handy on numerous occasions. (It is also illustrative of how flexible InDesign's tables can be and how easy they are to script sometimes.) You select the cells to be summed and the cell in which the sum is to be placed, and run the script. In the table below, the selection is indicated by shading; when the script is run, the sum of the values in the selection is placed in the cell next to TOTAL.

One	Two
Pencils	12345
Biros	678
Paper	9101
Toner	23
TOTAL	

In the example here, the last cell is empty and will be filled with the sum of the four cells above it. If there's anything in that last cell, it will be replaced with the new value. (As it stands, the script handles decimals if they're dots but not thousands separators.) Here is the script:

```
if (app.selection[0].constructor.name != 'Cell') exit();
var myNumbers = app.selection[0].contents;
var mySum = 0;
for (var i = 0; i < myNumbers.length-1; i++) {
 mySum += Number (myNumbers[i]);
}
app.selection[0].cells[-1].contents = String (sum);
```

With a number of cells selected, `app.selection[0].contents` returns an array. As JavaScript always returns cell content as a string, before adding any cell content to the sum it should be converted to a number (using JavaScript's `Number()` function). At the same time, you must enter a string value in a cell's contents, so the sum must be converted to a string before being entered in the last cell.

Processing all tables in a document

To process all tables, we need to find every table in every story:

```
app.activeDocument.stories.everyItem().tables.everyItem();
```

In fact, we want to process columns, which we can refer to collectively as follows:

```
app.activeDocument.stories.everyItem().tables.everyItem().
columns.everyItem();
```

The script that snaps all columns in all tables can now be stated like this:

```
var myColumns = app.activeDocument.stories.everyItem().tables.
everyItem().
   columns.everyItem().getElements();
   for (var i = 0; i < myColumns.length; i++) {
   snapColumn (myColumns[i]);
   }
```

The call to `snapColumn`, naturally, is a call to the function we defined earlier that snaps the column in one table.

Applying table styles

Table styles are flexible tools to format tables, but they have a drawback. In a table style you can assign separate cell styles to the table header, footer, and body. This is fine if you create new tables and set a table header and footer, but it's no good for existing tables that come in with a document imported from Word, for instance. So you have to apply the table style to the table, then the header style to the cells in the top row and the footer cell style to the cells in the last row. This can be tedious, and a script can sort this out quickly.

In the next example I assume that you have a table style called 'Standard' and three cell styles, 'Standard body', 'Standard top', and 'Standard bottom'. To apply the styles to all tables in your document, use this script:

```
try {
  var myDoc = app.activeDocument;
  var myTables = myDoc.stories.everyItem().tables.everyItem().
getElements();
  for (var i = 0; i < myTables.length; i++) {
    myTables[i].appliedTableStyle = 'Standard';
    myTables[i].rows[0].cells.everyItem().appliedCellStyle =
'Standard top';
    myTables[i].rows[-1].cells.everyItem().appliedCellStyle =
'Standard bottom';
  }
} catch (_) { }
```

Note the extensive use of `everyItem()` in the script: tables process much quicker this way.

Find and change in tables only

Earlier we mentioned that in the interface it's not possible to restrict finding and replacing to tables. That limitation is easy to get around with a script. Suppose that you want to replace the paragraph style 'Normal' with the style 'Table', only, naturally, in tables. This is the script:

```
app.findTextPreferences = app.changeTextPreferences = null;
app.findTextPreferences.appliedParagraphStyle = 'Normal';
app.changeTextPreferences.appliedParagraphStyle = 'Table';
app.activeDocument.stories.everyItem().tables.everyItem().
changeText();
```

16

Text Frames and Rectangles

Some aspects of text frames are relatively easy in scripting. We'll go into enough of these straightforward properties and methods here so that you can do some useful things with text frames. It's easier to start with an existing text frame, so start a new document and add a text frame.

Script label/name

Page items can be labelled in two ways. The original method, which was the only method up to and including CS5, is to use the `label` property, which is the equivalent of setting the item's script label in the Script Label panel (Window > Utilities > Script Label). In JavaScript you set it as follows:

```
app.activeDocument.textFrames[0].label = 'test';
```

You can check in the Script Label panel that the frame has been labelled. To test whether a frame has a particular label, use this:

```
if (myFrame.label == 'test') {
 . . .
}
```

From CS6 you can use another method, namely, to name page items on the Layers panel. You do this by setting the item's **name** property:

```
app.activeDocument.textFrames[0].name = 'test';
```

Using the name property is more useful than the label property because you can now get a reference to the page item very quickly:

```
myFrame = app.activeDocument.textFrames.item ('test');
```

Frame dimensions

Let's start with the frame's position and size. Looking through **textFrame**'s properties, you'll come across **geometricBounds**. This looks promising; let's find out what it is. Select the text frame, then in ESTK's console type the following line and press Enter:

```
app.selection[0].geometricBounds;
```

To our query the ESTK responds with four numbers, e.g. **149,109,324,305** (measurement units are points here). Four numbers – what kind of object is that? We'll find out:

```
app.selection[0].geometricBounds.constructor.name;
```

which prompts the ESTK to respond **Array**. So the geometric bounds of a text frame are stored in an array with four numbers. You'll understand that the numbers in that array correspond in some way with the numbers you see in the Transform panel, but they're not exactly the same. The screenshot in **FIGURE 10** shows our text frame and the Transform panel next to it.

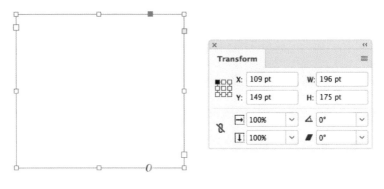

FIGURE 10

Make sure that you select the top-left reference point in the Transform panel. Comparing the values in the Transform panel and the values in the array returned by `geometricBounds`, you see that the panel tells you the horizontal (X) and vertical (Y) coordinates of the selected reference point and the width (W) and height (H) of the text frame. The geometric bounds, on the other hand, always return the frame's top, left, bottom, and right position, in that order. The selected reference point plays no role.

As we're dealing with an array, we can access any of the four individual values in the normal way: `myFrame.geometricBounds[0]` is the frame's top, `myFrame.geometricBounds[1]` is the frame's left side, etc. Though the bounds don't specify the frame's width and height, these can be easily calculated: a frame's width is `myFrame.geometricBounds[3] – myFrame.geometricBounds[1]`: the difference between the frame's right- and left-hand sides.

Resizing a frame

The geometric bounds of a textframe can be changed to change the frame's position and size. For example, to change the size of our text frame, run this line:

```
// Original bounds are 149,109,324,305
app.activeDocument.textFrames.itemByName ('test').geometricBounds
= [149,109,344,325];
```

The result is that the frame is 20 units taller and wider, while the coordinates of the top-left corner don't change. So what you do is simply to feed the frame an array of numbers. You could even move a frame by increasing or decreasing all four values in the array by the same amount, but there are better methods for moving frames.

Moving a frame

Again consulting the OMV, you notice that there is a method `move()`. This method can be used in several different ways: move a frame either by given amounts or move it to a certain position on the same page; move a frame to a different page; or move a frame to a different layer. To move a frame to a certain position on the same page, use this form:

```
myFrame.move ([10, 12]);
```

This uses the document's units of measurement. To use specific units, e.g. millimetres, use this form:

```
myFrame.move (['10 mm', '12 mm']);
```

The position to which the frame should be moved is given as an array of two numbers, the horizontal and the vertical position (it is a bit confusing that the geometric bounds use the order vertical-horizontal, and `move()` horizontal-vertical). This is always the frame's top-left point.

To move a frame *by* a certain amount, for example, 10 millimetres to the right and 16 down, use this:

```
myFrame.move (undefined, ['10 mm', '16 mm']);
```

(To move frames up or to the left, use negative values.) This funny construction is necessary because when `move()` is used with one parameter (and that parameter is an array of two numbers), it's interpreted as 'move to'. The `move()` method in fact has two parameters, its second is interpreted as 'move by'. As we don't want to specify the first parameter we use 'undefined' instead. A bit Jabberwockyish but that's how it works.

To move a frame to a different page, say, page 4, use this:

```
var myDoc = app.activeDocument;
myDoc.textFrames.itemByName ('test').move (myDoc.pages[3]);
```

And to move a frame to a different layer, say, 'captions', use this:

```
var myDoc = app.activeDocument;
myDoc.textFrames.itemByName('test').move (myDoc.layers.
item('captions'));
// Alternative:
myDoc.textFrames.itemByName('test').itemLayer = myDoc.layers.
item('captions');
```

(layers is a property of the document object.) It's not possible to combine any of these move operations: to move a frame to a certain position on a different page and to a different layer, you need to move that frame three times. Note that when you move an item to a different page, it is always positioned in the top-left corner of that page. To move it to the same position on the target page, first record the frame's geometric bounds, move it, then reapply the bounds:

```
var myDoc = app.activeDocument;
var myFrame = myDoc.textFrames.itemByName ('test');
var gb = myFrame.geometricBounds;
myFrame.move (myDoc.pages[3]);
myFrame.geometricBounds = gb;
myFrame.move (myDoc.layers.item('captions'));
```

Creating a frame

To add a text frame to the active document, use this line:

```
app.activeDocument.textFrames.add();
```

Where is this frame created? If you don't tell the script where to put it, the frame is created in the top-left corner of the first page, 10 points high and wide (irrespective of the document's measurement units). Can we change this behaviour? For one thing, we can tell the script to create the frame on a specific page:

```
app.activeDocument.pages[3].textFrames.add();
```

We can then use the frame's geometric bounds to change its size and position:

```
var myFrame = app.activeDocument.pages[3].textFrames.add();
myFrame.geometricBounds = ['30pt', '30pt', '300pt', '200pt'];
```

Note that in the first line we create a variable, `myFrame`, and assign a new text frame to it in one statement. In the second line we set the geometric bounds. We could also add some text to the new frame, and while we're at it, we'll add a label or a name, too:

```
myFrame.contents = 'It was a dark and stormy night.';
myFrame.name = 'test';
```

This adds plain, unformatted, text to the text frame. It can be formatted with styles using the various methods outlined earlier.

A text frame's page number

An elusive property is 'page number'. Looking hard in the OMV under the **page** object you expect a property like `pageNumber` or just `number` or `folio`, but it's not there. In fact, it's the name of a page:

```
myTextFrame.parentPage.name;
```

All page items have a property `parentPage`, and the `Page` object, like almost all objects, has the property `name`. The page number that's returned may include a section prefix, depending on the setting in the Numbering and Section Options dialog.

Keep in mind that the page number (or 'folio') is what is printed on the page. If you want to know the page's rank in the document (the 'how-many-th'), you use the page's document offset:

```
myTextFrame.parentPage.documentOffset;
```

If this returns 10, then the frame is on the document's 11th page, no matter what the printed page number is.

Graphics

When you place an image in InDesign, it is typically placed in a rectangle. You can verify this in the usual way: place an image, select it, then type `app.selection[0]` in the ESTK's console and press Enter/Return. The ESTK responds with `[object Rectangle]`. Rectangles are similar to text frames in several ways: for example, their size and position is stored in the same geometric bounds. Text frames and rectangles also share properties such as `name`, `label`, and `stroke`, and methods such as `move()`. The only difference, naturally, is their contents: text frames contain text, rectangles contain images.

Captions

To round off this section on text frames and rectangles, let's look at captions. I find InDesign's (automatic) captions a bit unwieldy, and I for one prefer to script captions. A caption, naturally, is just a text frame positioned in relation to a picture. Take the photograph and its caption in **FIGURE 11**.

FIGURE 11

The caption is a text frame whose left and right sides are the same as the photograph's; the caption's top coincides with the photograph's bottom; the caption's bottom is a given distance from its top. The way I place captions like these is as follows: I place a photograph, then I place a text frame for the caption and add the caption text. Then I select the photograph and the caption (in that order) and run the following script (I assume the presence of an object style 'Caption', in which among other things, Auto-Sizing, Height Only is enabled.):

```
if (app.selection.length !== 2
   && app.selection[0].constructor.name != 'Rectangle'
   && app.selection[1].constructor.name != 'TextFrame') {
     exit();
}


var myPicture = app.selection[0];
var myCaption = app.selection[1];
var gb = myPicture.geometricBounds;
// Set position and size of the caption
myCaption.geometricBounds = [gb[2], gb[1], gb[2]+14, gb[3]];
// Apply object style to the caption -- we assume it's present
myCaption.applyObjectStyle (app.activeDocument.objectStyles.
item('Caption'));
// Group the picture and the caption
myPicture.parentPage.groups.add ([myPicture, myCaption]);
```

We first check if it's safe to continue, which we define here as 'the selection is two objects, the first one a rectangle, the second, a text frame'. We then bind the selected rectangle to a variable, myPicture; and the text frame to myCaption. Then we assign the photograph's geometric bounds to a variable, gb (we need to refer to this variable several times so we keep its name short).

The next step is to position and size the caption's frame on the basis of the picture's geometric bounds. The caption's left and right side are easy, they correspond with the picture's left and right sides, gb[1] and gb[3], respectively. The caption's top coincides with the picture's bottom, gb[2]. Finally, we set the caption's height arbitrarily to 14 points, so its bottom corresponds with the picture's bottom plus 14, or **gb[2]+14**. The object style's Auto-Size sizes the caption precisely. That gives us all the values needed to set the caption's position and size:

```
myCaption.geometricBounds = [gb[2], gb[1], gb[2]+14, gb[3]];
```

We assume that the document's default measurement is points. If it's not, either set it to points or change **14** to a size appropriate to your units of measurement.

The last steps are to assign an object style to the caption and group it with the picture. Naturally, we place the group on the picture's parent page. Though it's not necessary to group the caption and the picture, it does make them easier to handle.

17

Resources

Some good resources are available from Adobe. As mentioned elsewhere in this guide, documentation on the ESTK is available in the application itself via Help > JavaScript Tools Guide, chapter 2. In those same Help menus in the ESTK you'll find introductions to scripting: Adobe Intro to Scripting.

Apart from the present title, there are five book publications on scripting InDesign with JavaScript:

– InDesign automatisieren: Keine Angst vor Skripting, GREP & Co (Gregor Fellenz; in German). This title covers both JavaScript and GREP. The second edition appeared in 2015; an English translation is in preparation (writing early 2019).

– Automating Adobe InDesign CS4 with ExtendScript (Shirley Hopkins). It has CS4 in the title but most of the contents covers the latest versions of InDesign as well.

– InDesign CS5 Automation Using XML & JavaScript (Grant Gamble) Especially useful for scripting XML. This book has CS5 in its title but is still relevant for the latest InDesign versions. A more advanced book than the present book.

- InDesign CS5 JavaScript (Grant Gamble) This is the same as the previous title without the XML chapters.
- A guide to ScriptUI, the module included in the ESTK to write dialogs for all CS/CC applications.

An excellent user-to-user forum for scripters is the one hosted by Adobe. InDesignSecrets, too, has a good forum. If you know German, a good forum is HilfDirSelbst.

The number of sites with useful information on InDesign scripting and with example scripts is growing. I maintain an annotated list on my web site.

An alternative to the ESTK's object-model viewer is provided by Gregor Fellenz.

You can reach me at p.kahrel@gmail.com.

Printed in Great Britain
by Amazon

40801893R00078